P9-EBY-618

Pelican Books

Advisory Editor for Linguistics: David Crystal

Grammar

F. R. Palmer was educated at Bristol Grammar School and
New College, Oxford. From 1950 to 1960 he was Lecturer in
Linguistics at the School of Oriental and African Studies,
University of London, where he undertook research into
Ethiopian languages. In 1952 he spent a year in Ethiopia
studying that country's languages – Tigrinya, Tigre, Bilin and
Agaw. He became Professor of Linguistics at University
College, Bangor, in 1960, and in 1965 he was appointed
Professor of Linguistic Science at the University of Reading.
He has lectured in most European countries, in North and
South America, as well as in Morocco, Tunisia, Indonesia
and Uganda.

Professor Palmer has been chairman of the Linguistics
Association and is the present editor of the *Journal of
Linguistics*. His publications include *The Morphology of the
Tigre Noun* and *A Linguistic Study of the English Verb*.

Grammar

Frank Palmer

Penguin Books

Penguin Books Ltd, Harmondsworth,
Middlesex, England
Penguin Books Inc., 7110 Ambassador Road,
Baltimore, Maryland 21207, U.S.A.
Penguin Books Australia Ltd, Ringwood,
Victoria, Australia

First published 1971
Copyright © Frank Palmer, 1971

Made and printed in Great Britain by
Hazell Watson & Viney Ltd,
Aylesbury, Bucks
Set in Monotype Times Roman

Contents

1. Grammar and Grammars

'The question is,' said Alice, 'whether you can make words mean different things.'

'The question is,' said Humpty Dumpty, 'which is to be master – that's all.'

Alice was much too puzzled to say anything, so after a minute Humpty Dumpty began again. 'They've a temper most of them – particularly verbs, they're the proudest – adjectives you can do anything with, but not verbs – however, I can manage the whole lot! Impenetrability! That's what I say!'

LEWIS CARROLL. *Through the Looking-Glass.*

1.1 Why study grammar?

Alice had almost certainly learnt some grammar at school. It is almost equally certain that she was bored by it. In more recent times most school children have been spared the boredom because the teaching of grammar has been dropped from the syllabus and, unlike Alice, they may well never know the difference between an adjective and a verb.

Yet this is an extraordinary and quite deplorable state of affairs. Few areas of our experience are closer to us or more continuously with us than our language. We spend a large part of our waking life speaking, listening, reading and writing. The central part of a language (its 'mechanics', its 'calculus' – other metaphors will do) is its grammar, and this should be of vital interest to any intelligent educated person. If it has not been of such interest, then the fault must be in the way in which it has been presented, or in the failure to recognize its importance within this essentially human activity, language.

Man is not well defined as *homo sapiens* ('man with wisdom').

For what do we mean by wisdom? More recently anthropologists have talked about 'man the tool-maker', but apes too can make primitive tools. What sets man apart from the rest of the animal kingdom is his ability to speak; he is 'man the speaking animal' – *homo loquens*. But it is grammar that makes language so essentially a human characteristic. For though other creatures can make meaningful sounds, the link between sound and meaning is for them of a far more primitive kind than it is for man, and the link for man is grammar. Man is not merely *homo loquens*; he is *homo grammaticus*.

We can see this point more clearly if we look briefly at the idea of communication. Men have for centuries been interested in the language they speak but only in recent years have they attempted to examine it in an objective or 'scientific' way. Some scholars, in their resolve to look at language without prejudice and preconception, have begun with the premise that language is a communication system and as such can and must be compared with other communication systems. Some such systems are those used by animals. The gibbons, for instance, have at least nine different calls. The bees have a complicated system of dances to indicate the direction, the distance and the quantity of newly discovered nectar. Other systems are mechanical; traffic lights, for instance, use three different colours, but give four different signals (in some countries five, where green as well as red combines with amber). All of these seem to have something in common with language. They all have something to communicate and they all have their own ways of communicating it.

Can we say that these communication systems have grammars – and if not, why not? The study of these other systems has not proved to be very helpful in the detailed understanding of language, though it has helped us to see the ways in which language differs from them. The main difference here is the enormous complexity of language, and it is within this complexity that we must look for grammar. A gibbon call has merely a meaning such as 'danger' or 'food', and there are only nine or so different calls. The bees can tell only the direction, the distance and the amount of the nectar. The traffic lights can only signal 'stop', 'go', etc. But the possible sentences of English with all the possible meanings are myriad or, more probably, infinite in number. We do not learn the meaning of each of all these count-less sentences separately. This is shown by the fact that many, if not most, of the sentences we produce or hear are new, in the sense that they are not identical with sentences that we have produced or heard before (and some have never been produced or heard by anyone), yet we understand their meaning. There is a highly complex system in their construction, and this complex system differs from language to language – that is why languages are different. Within this system there is a complex set of rela-tions that link the sounds of the language (or its written symbols) with the 'meanings', the message they have to convey.

In the widest sense of the term, grammar IS that complex set of relations. According to a recent definition, grammar is 'a device that specifies the infinite set of well-formed sentences and assigns to each of them one or more structural descriptions'. That is to say it tells us just what are all the possible sentences of a language and provides a description of them. This is no small task, but one that is well worthy of human study.

It is a sad fact that we are very ignorant of some important aspects of speech. We have very little idea of the steps by which men came to speak and, indeed, no accurate assessment of the time at which speech began. At some time in the past man de-veloped his speech organs; these were originally designed for eat-ing and breathing, but became highly specialized for the purpose of speech. We do not know when or how this took place, for the organs are all of flesh and do not survive in fossil remains. Only very little can be conjectured from the shape of the jaw. In any case, if we knew how and when these organs developed this would tell us only how man came to master the sounds of language. It would tell us nothing about the development of the grammatical systems. The evidence of these goes back only as far as we have written records, a mere few thousand years, a tiny fraction of the total time that man has been speaking.

We are ignorant too of the neuro-physiological mechanisms that make speech, and grammar in particular, possible. We know that speech is normally located in the left hemisphere of the brain, though it is a remarkable fact that if this part is damaged in early childhood speech is still developed. Since in such cases another part of the brain is used it would seem that no part of the brain is especially adapted for speech.

There are three characteristics of language that are important for the understanding of the nature of grammar: it is complex, productive and arbitrary.

That language is highly complex is shown by the fact that up to now it has not proved possible to translate mechanically from one language to another, with really satisfactory results. Some stories, as, for instance, the one of the computer that translated 'out of sight, out of mind' as 'invisible idiot', are no doubt apocryphal, but it is true that the best programmed computer still cannot consistently translate from, say, Russian into English. The fault lies not in the computer but in the failure to provide it with sufficiently accurate instructions, because we are still unable to handle this vastly complex system. It has been suggested, moreover, that from what we know about language and the human brain speech ought to be impossible. For it has been calculated that if the brain used any of the known methods of computing language, it would take several minutes to produce or to understand a single short sentence! Part of the task of the grammarian is, then, to unravel the complexities of languages, and, as far as possible, simplify them. Yet total description of a language is an impossibility at present and even in the foreseeable future.

Secondly, language is productive. We can produce myriads of sentences that we have never heard or uttered before. Many of the sentences in this book have been produced for the first time, yet they are intelligible to the reader. More strikingly, if I produce a sentence with completely new words, e.g. *Lishes rop pibs* and assure the reader that this is a real English sentence he will be able to produce a whole set of other sentences or sentence fragments based upon it, e.g. *Pibs are ropped by lishes*, *A lish ropping pibs*, etc. It is clear that we have some kind of sentence-producing mechanism – that sentences are produced anew each time and not merely imitated. One task of grammatical theory is to explain this quite remarkable fact. As we shall see, many grammatical theories have failed in this, but one solution is considered in the final chapter.

Thirdly, language is arbitrary. There is no one-to-one relation between sound and meaning. This accounts for the fact that languages differ, and they differ most of all in their grammatical structure. But how far are these differences only superficial, in the shape of the words and their overt patterns? Some scholars would maintain that 'deep down' there are strong similarities – even 'universal' characteristics, disguised by the superficial features of sound (and perhaps of meaning). It is not at all clear how we can find the answer to this problem. When we discuss grammar, however, we do assume that many characteristics of language are shared. For this reason we talk of 'nouns', of 'verbs', of 'gender' or of 'number' and other such grammatical categories. These are discussed in detail in the next section.

1.2 What is grammar?

There is a great deal of confusion about grammar because of the very many different ways in which the term is used in ordinary speech. Let us take a brief look at some of them. All of the following I would regard as misconceptions.

1. *A grammar of a language is a book written about it.* The word 'grammar' is often used to refer to the book itself – school children may often ask 'May I borrow your grammar?' It is obvious, of course, that a grammar in this sense means a grammar book, a book ABOUT grammar, but there is a real danger that even if this is accepted, it may still be thought that, even if the grammar is not the book itself, it is at least what is in the book. But in this sense the grammar of the language is no more than the grammar as presented by the author of the book.

2. *The grammar of the language is found only in the written language – spoken languages have no grammar or at least fluctuate so much that they are only partially grammatical.* This viewpoint has been supported by the etymology of the word 'grammar' – it comes from the Greek word meaning 'to write'. This is an

important widespread belief, and I shall spend a whole section considering it (1.4, p. 26). It is enough to comment here that in this sense languages which have never been written down would be said to have no grammar. But this we cannot accept.

3. *Some languages have grammar, others do not: Chinese, for instance, has no grammar, and English has precious little.* What is meant by this is that English has very few 'inflections' – that each word has only a few different shapes and that in Chinese all the words keep the same shape. Whereas in Latin the verb *amo*: 'I love' has over one hundred different forms, the English verb 'to love' has only four forms: *love*, *loves*, *loved* and *loving* (some verbs have five: *take*, *takes*, *took*, *taken*, *taking*), and the Chinese word for 'love' is always the same. But this is to use the term 'grammar' in a very restricted sense. It refers to MORPHOLOGY only, to the actual forms of the words, and it omits altogether the syntax, the way in which the words are put together (these are roughly the traditional definitions of morphology, or inflection, and syntax). But the order of words is a matter of syntax and syntax is a part of grammar (see 2.2). A very important part of English grammar tells us that *John saw Bill* is different from *Bill saw John* and that *a steel sheet* is different from *sheet steel*; yet in the restricted sense of grammar that we are now considering, these differences would not be deemed grammatical.

4. *Grammar is something that can be good or bad, correct or incorrect. It is bad (incorrect) grammar to say 'It's me', for instance.* This again is a widespread belief and also deserves careful consideration (see 1.3). Once again, however, notice that on this interpretation it will usually be languages that are formally taught in school or through books that are said to have any grammar. For it is at school or in books that we usually find the criteria for what is good and what is bad grammar.

5. *Some people know the grammar of their language, others do not.* This is a little more subtle. It implies that a language does not have a grammar until it is made explicit and can be learnt from a grammar book or at school. But there is surely a sense in which knowing the grammar of a language means that you can speak it grammatically. An Englishman might well be said to

know the grammar of French perfectly if he spoke it as grammatically as a Frenchman, but had never attended a class or read a book about French.

It is fairly obvious from all this that I want to use the word 'grammar' in the sense suggested at the end of the last sentence. It describes what people do when they speak their language; it is not something that has to be found in books, written down or learnt by heart. As investigators, of course, we DO want to write down, i.e. write about the grammar of a language; but writing it down does not bring it into existence any more than writing about biology creates living cells!

Within linguistics, 'grammar' is normally used in a technical sense to distinguish it chiefly from phonology, the study of the sounds of a language, and semantics, the study of meaning. It lies so to speak 'in the middle', between these two, and is related in a Janus-like way to both. There is some debate still about the precise status of grammar vis-à-vis the other 'levels', as we shall see particularly in the last chapter.

Among some scholars the term 'grammar' is used in a rather wider sense to include, to some degree, both phonology and semantics (see especially pp. 185–6) with the term 'syntax' used for the central portion. But I use the term in the narrower, more traditional sense, and this book contains therefore no detailed discussion of sound systems or of meaning.

1.3 Correct and incorrect

In the previous section I mentioned the view that grammar can be good or bad, correct or incorrect. This might seem reasonable enough. Is grammar not like manners which can and should be the subject of approval or disapproval? This view is very widespread and is, of course, related to the other views that were discussed – that grammar is something that can or must be learnt from a book, and that knowing the grammar of a language means having an explicit knowledge of it. Some years ago, for instance, I lived in Wales and made an attempt to learn the Welsh language. One of my Welsh friends on hearing this commented

'You'll learn to speak better Welsh than we do – you'll have learnt the grammar.' The implications are clear: there is a better and a worse kind of Welsh and the better kind is to be found in grammar books – it can be learnt and so 'known'.

These misconceptions are all mixed together, but the basic mistake is seeing grammar as a set of NORMATIVE rules – rules that tell us how we ought to speak and write. It is important incidentally to stress the word 'normative', since as we shall see later one theory of grammar is exclusively in terms of rules; these will prove however to be *de*scriptive rules (rules that describe the language), not *pre*scriptive rules (rules that prescribe the language). That is, they will be rules that state what we do in fact say, not rules that state what we ought to say.

Normative grammar teaches us to say *It is I* instead of *It's me*, to avoid ending sentences with prepositions, to know the difference between *owing to* and *due to*, to use *each other* instead of *one another* when only two people are involved, and so on. The authority of these 'correct' forms lies, of course, in the grammar books. They have been drilled into generations of schoolboys and it is no coincidence that we speak of the 'grammar' schools. In France there is an even more impressive authority, the French Academy, which since 1635 has been the body with the right to decide what is and what is not permissible in the French language.

Most of these rules of grammar have no real justification and there is therefore no serious reason for condemning the 'errors' they prescribe. What is correct and what is not correct is ultimately only a matter of what is accepted by society, for language is a matter of conventions within society. If everyone says *It's me*, then surely *It's me* is correct English. (For by what criterion can EVERYONE within a society be guilty of bad grammar?) But we must be a little careful here. It is not simply a matter that whatever is said is thereby correct; I am not arguing that 'anything goes'. It depends on who says it and when. In other words, there ARE manners even in language. Certain language forms are regarded as uneducated or vulgar; this is a judgement that our society makes. Some forms of language are acceptable in certain situations only. At an interview for a job, for instance, we have to watch our language as well as our clothes. To use certain types of language there would be as detrimental as wearing old clothes. But most of the rules of the 'traditional' grammar that has been taught over the years are not rules of behaviour of this kind. They prescribe forms that many of us would never normally use, and if we do we feel we are 'speaking like a book'. The best way of seeing that these rules have no validity is to look at the justification or supposed justification that is given for them.

First of all, many of the rules are essentially rules taken from Latin. Latin was the classical language known by all educated people and was once regarded as the model for all other languages. Even today there are people who say that Latin is more 'logical' than English. In the debate a few years ago about the teaching of Latin at school and the requirement of Latin for entrance to Oxford and Cambridge, the familiar arguments were put forward – Latin helped to discipline the mind, Latin taught the students grammar. This latter statement was true in a rather paradoxical way. Since most English grammar teaching was based upon Latin the students were often at a loss. They could not see why English had a subjunctive or a dative case, but when they learnt Latin it all became clear. Latin helped them with their English grammar, but only because English grammar was really Latin grammar all the time!

The rule that we should say *It is I* is a typical example of a Latin rule taken over for English. The argument (which I do not accept) runs as follows. In Latin the nouns have six different cases as exemplified by:

nominative	*mensa*	*amicus*
vocative	*mensa*	*amice*
accusative	*mensam*	*amicum*
genitive	*mensae*	*amici*
dative	*mensae*	*amico*
ablative	*mensa*	*amico*
	('table')	('friend')[1]

1. In this chapter I use a number of technical or semi-technical terms because it is unavoidable in this discussion. An account of the way in which they are used is to be found in Chapter 2.

With the verb 'to be' the rule is that the complement must be in the same case as the subject. If therefore we translate *Caesar* (subject) *is my friend* (complement) the word for *Caesar* is in the nominative (subjects of finite verbs are always in the nominative) and so are the words for *my friend*. Thus we have *Caesar est amicus meus*. The same is true of pronouns, so that we find in one of the plays of Plautus, *Ego sum tu, tu es ego*, literally *I am thou, thou art I*. On the analogy of Latin, English *I* is said to be nominative and *me* accusative. Since in *It is . . . It* is also nominative as it is the subject of the sentence, it follows that we can say only *It is I* and that *It is me* is 'ungrammatical'.

The same kind of argument is used to prescribe the 'correct' reply to *Who's there?* In Latin the answer would again be in the nominative – the same case as the word for *Who*; in English we are, therefore, expected to say *I* not *me*. This reasoning also accounts for the rule that we should say *He is bigger than I*, not *He is bigger than me*. In Latin the noun being compared has to be in the same case as the noun with which it is compared, and since *He* is in the nominative so too must *I* be. (But we have to say *He hit a man bigger than me* because *a man* is the object and is in the accusative.)

There is no reason at all why English should follow the Latin rule. In the first place English has no case endings for the noun (except possibly the genitive) and only a vestige of case with the pronoun – *I/me, he/him, she/her, we/us, they/them*. Secondly, though there is this rule in Latin, there are contrary rules in other languages. In French, forms that are literally *It's I, . . . bigger than I* are quite ungrammatical: we cannot say **C'est je*, or **plus grand que je*. *Je* cannot stand alone. French here uses the form *moi. C'est moi, plus grand que moi*. There is a story of an important conference at which it was asked if there was an Englishman present who spoke fluent French and one man raised his hand and cried 'Je!' *Moi* is not quite equivalent to English *me*, because French has an object (accusative) form *me* also, but the point is made – French does NOT allow the nominative form in these constructions. In Arabic, more strikingly, the verb 'to be' actually requires the accusative to follow it (like any other verb).

If we had chosen Arabic as our ideal, *It's I* would have been as ungrammatical as **He hit I*, and *It's me* the form prescribed! (It is a convention to mark forms that do not occur with an asterisk.)

Strangely enough, those who advocate these rules do not simply admit they take them from Latin. They produce specious arguments in their favour. For *It is I* it is argued that since *I* is identical with *it* they must be in the same case. This is still seriously put forward sometimes, but it is utterly implausible. Is *myself* then in the nominative in *I washed myself*? Perhaps there is some feeling that there is a kind of identity or equality, as in arithmetic where $2 + 2 = 4$, but even so, what has this to do with the choice of case? A different argument is put forward for *He is bigger than I*. It is argued that *than* is a conjunction, not a preposition, and that this sentence is short for *He is bigger than I am, am* being 'understood'. But this will not work either. By the same token we could argue that we ought to say **He came after I* on the grounds that *after* also is a conjunction and that this sentence is short for *He came after I did*. The arguments are identical, yet no one argues for *He came after I*. Why not? The answer is simple. In Latin there is a preposition *post* meaning *after* as well as a conjunction *postquam*, but the word meaning *than* (*quam*), is always a conjunction and never a preposition. But why should this be true of English? Should we not rather treat *than* in the same way as *after* (either preposition or conjunction) and permit

> He came after me.
> He came after I did.
> He is bigger than me.
> He is bigger than I am.

The trouble with rules like these is that people do not understand them and often misapply them. This has, for instance, become almost a maxim in English: 'When in doubt use *I* not *me*.' This is the reason for the very common occurrence today of *between you and I* and similar expressions, where *between you and me* would be 'grammatical'. As a linguist I make no judgement; perhaps *I* is now the form that is used after *and* – there would be nothing strange linguistically about this.

A rule of a quite different kind that has come from Latin is the rule that we must not end a sentence with a preposition or, facetiously, that a preposition is a word you must never end a sentence with. In fact it is true that Latin does not permit sentences with final prepositions, and it is even true that 'form' words, as they are often called, like prepositions and conjunctions, are not permitted at the end of a line of verse, even when this is not the end of a sentence. But again why should this be imposed upon English? It is easy enough to make fun of this rule. It is said that one of Winston Churchill's papers was altered by a secretary to avoid ending a sentence with a preposition and Churchill, restoring the preposition to its original place, wrote 'This is the kind of pedantry up with which I will not put', and there is the story of a little girl who finding her mother had brought up a book that she did not like, said 'What did you bring that book I didn't want to be read to out of up for?'

There is, then, no reason why the grammar of English should be based upon the grammar of Latin or upon the grammar of any other language. Similarly, we should never expect the grammar of any other language to be based upon that of English. It is the assumption that other languages will be like our own in their grammatical structures (as well as in their sound system and their semantics) that makes it so difficult for people to learn foreign languages. At a very early age we become conditioned to thinking that our own language does things in the 'right' or the 'natural' way and that there is something rather odd about the way other languages work. Even if we do not seriously believe it, we may well feel that the word *dog* is more appropriate to the four-legged pet than French *chien* or German *Hund*. In Aldous Huxley's *Crome Yellow* there is a sequence in which a character gazing at some pigs wallowing in the mud remarks 'Rightly is they called pigs.' The grammarian Jespersen has a similar story of a little girl who made the exciting discovery that pigs are called pigs 'because they are such swine'.

Clearly none of this can be taken seriously, but in grammar the preconceptions are more deeply rooted. Consider, for instance, the fact that in English the subject of a sentence normally precedes the verb, and the object normally follows, that in *John hit Bill* we know that John did the hitting and Bill was the one who was hit. There is no logical or natural reason why this should be so; in a language like Latin which marks subjects and objects by different endings on the nouns the order of the words is not a crucial fact in the meaning. The Latin sentence *Marcum vidit Caesar* (even if slightly unusual Latin) means *Caesar saw Marcus* and not *Marcus saw Caesar* (which would require the forms *Marcus* and *Caesarem*). Similarly it is not a universal feature of languages to ask questions by changing the order of part of the sentence, as in English we have the statement *John can go* and the question *Can John go?* Some languages merely use intonation to indicate questions, but many have a word or particle that indicates them (Latin has the suffix *-ne*, Tigrinya, an Ethiopian language, has the suffix *-do*). In Welsh, however, the normal order of words in STATEMENTS is to put the auxiliary verb first, then the subject and then the main verb. Thus *He is going* is *Mae ef yn mynd* (literally, I suppose, **Is he in going*). An English child who had to learn Welsh came home complaining bitterly that it was a very stupid language because 'every time they want to say something, they ask a question'! At a quite early age he had completely accepted a conventional device for English as a universal fact of all languages.

It is unfortunate, perhaps, that French forms its questions in a way similar to that of English, so that *Have you seen ...?* is *Avez-vous vu ...?* For French is the language that is most commonly learnt by English-speaking children, and it seems clear that the occurrence of the same device in French can only strengthen the feeling that it is wholly natural. Worse, it occurs also in German, and German is the second language most commonly taught in schools. This method of forming questions is not, then, a purely English convention, but it is only a Western European convention and the fact that it turns up in all three of these languages is a result of cultural contact over the centuries. But it is in no sense natural or universal.

Many traditional grammar books of foreign languages have taken it for granted that all languages have the same grammar, and usually it has been Latin grammar. In this spirit one grammarian remarked that Japanese was defective in the gerund – all respectable languages, it would seem, must have gerunds!

There are scholars today who believe that there are *universal features* in the grammars of all languages. But these features are of an abstract kind, in what is called 'deep structure' (see p. 142). The more obvious features of the grammars of different languages, those that are on the 'surface', e.g. the formation of the plurals, the order of the words, the case used after the verb BE, vary from language to language. To expect English to follow Latin in these respects is simply preposterous.

A second source of normative rules is 'logic' – I use quotation marks because the arguments are often not logical at all. Sometimes this logic is invoked to justify a rule based on something else, e.g. Latin. We have seen an example of this in the justification of *It is I*. In English the most notorious example of the logical argument concerns double negatives. Why can't we say *I didn't see nobody* or *I didn't go nowhere*? Because, the answer will be, one negative 'cancels out' another, so that these two sentences really mean *I saw somebody* and *I went somewhere*. But this is nonsense. Why should two negatives cancel each other out? Why should they not reinforce each other? The 'logic' of this is presumably based on the mathematical rule that two minuses make a plus. This argument can be seen to be false if we look at other languages for in many of them double negatives are quite normal. They were in Anglo-Saxon and in earlier forms of English. They are in Spanish:

> *No dije nada* I said nothing (literally, Not I said nothing),

and in Russian:

> *nikto ne rabotal* No one worked (literally, Nobody not worked).

It was the same in classical Greek but not in Latin. This should be hardly surprising; if Latin had had double negatives they would have found favour, not disfavour, with English grammarians! There can, then, be no logical reason for excluding double negatives. No rules are broken by *I didn't see nobody*. It does *not* follow, however, that this sentence is 'good' English, if by 'good' we mean that spoken by educated people. Proving that there are no logical objections to double negatives does not show that they are acceptable in English. They are still (in the educated form of English) ungrammatical, in the sense that they do not conform to the accepted linguistic habits of the community. If, however, we hear someone say *I didn't see nobody* the only judgement we can rightly pass is that he is speaking a form of English (perhaps a dialect) of which we do not approve. We cannot rightly say that that dialect is any less logical than the dialect we ourselves speak.

Sometimes 'logic' is based upon a misinterpretation of the facts. Again, we have seen one example in the *He is bigger than I* argument – that *than* is a conjunction and that this is short for *than I am*. The argument collapses if we insist that *than* is a preposition too and so requires *me*. A similar false argument is found in the belief that there is something wrong with *Someone has left their book behind* – though the Duchess in *Alice in Wonderland* said 'If everybody minded their own business, the world would go round faster than it does.' How, we are asked, can the singular *someone* or *somebody* be referred to by the plural *their*? It should be *Someone has left his book behind*. The trouble is, of course, that it might be *her* book since *someone* does not distinguish sex as *his* and *her* do. So what can we do? Well, if we begin by rejecting the assumption that the sentence is ungrammatical we can say that *their* functions not only as the plural possessive but also as a singular possessive when sex is unknown (if sex is irrelevant *its* is used). Similarly, we find *they* as well as *he*, *she* and *it* used for the singular: *If anybody can come, would they please let me know*. This is a common and useful device; it is not illogical or ungrammatical unless we decide, contrary to our observations, that *they*, *them* and *their* are always plural.

If we turn to other languages the application of logic is even more dangerous and may often be a result simply of a false identification of the grammatical structure of that language with our own. For instance, in Tigrinya I can say what appears in word-for-word translation to be

> To-your-house I-come

or if I want to be more emphatic

> To-your-house I-am that-I-come.

But surely we might think this ought to be

> To-your-house it is that-I come
> (It is to your house that I come.)

But this bracketed sentence would not be a true translation, for there is emphasis not only on *to your house* but also on *I*: there is conflation of the notion *It is to your house that I am coming* and *It is I that am coming to your house*. Is it not then perfectly natural that *to-your-house* and *I-am* should both come outside the relative clause, leaving only *I come* inside? This neatly and conveniently combines the characteristics of the two English sentences. It is, of course, completely untranslatable word-for-word into English, but surely not any the less logical for that.

Another striking example of different logic in different languages concerns the use of singular forms with the numerals. English says *one dog*, but *five dogs*, *forty dogs*, etc., using the plural *dogs* with all the 'plural' numerals. But Welsh does not: we find *un ci* 'one dog', *pump ci* 'five dogs', *deugain ci* 'forty dogs' (*ci* is singular – the plural form of *ci* 'dog' is *cŵn*). In Tigre, an Ethiopian Semitic language, the same is true though with an added refinement. Many nouns are not true singulars, in their basic form, but collectives. An example would be *nəhab* 'bees'. In spite of the English translation this is not a plural – the plural is *änhab*. A 'pure' singular, which is better called the 'singulative', can be formed by the addition of a suffix – *nəhbät* 'a bee'. But while 'one bee' is, not surprisingly, *hätte nəhbät*, 'two bees' is *kəl'e nəhbät* and 'three bees' *säläs nəhbät*; paradoxically the singulative form HAS to be chosen with ALL the numerals, even those meaning more than one. There are many other languages which do the same. But are these less logical than English? The argument can go either way – either that we ought to use a plural form of the noun because the numeral shows that we have plural objects, or alternatively that we need not use the plural form because the numeral has already marked plurality and there is no point in marking it twice. It is English that is less economical here. It has what is usually called 'redundancy', marking what is already marked. (Another quite different example was pointed out to me by a Spanish friend. Why do we say *He put his hand in his pocket*? Why HIS hand, why HIS pocket? Do we seriously expect he put someone else's hand in someone else's pocket?)

A third source of normative rules is the belief that what used to be required in language still ought to be required, the older form being tacitly accepted as 'better'. This is probably the only argument in favour of *whom* rather than *who* in *Whom did you see?* when almost everyone would say *Who did you see? Whom* is virtually dead, but is kept alive artificially by the grammarians. In Bernard Shaw's *The Village Wooing*, the following conversation occurs:

If it doesn't matter who anybody marries, then it doesn't matter who I marry and it doesn't matter who you marry.
Whom, not who.
O, speak English: you're not on the telephone now.

This appeal to earlier forms of the language is particularly common in the discussion of meanings. When someone says, 'It really means . . .' they probably mean 'It used to mean . . .'. A very good example of this is found in the word *nice*, which some teachers still tell children really means 'precise' or 'exact' as in *a nice distinction* or *a nice point*. But this, except in these expressions, is what it *used* to mean, not what it means now. The trouble about appealing to older meanings is that there is no obvious time at which we can stop. For if we go back a little further we shall find that *nice* meant 'foolish' or 'simple', not far away in meaning from the Latin *nescius* 'ignorant', from which it is derived. But the Latin word comes from a negative prefix *ne-* and a root which, though it has the meaning 'to know' in Latin, originally meant 'to cut' and is related to *schism* and *shear*. So originally it should have had the meaning 'not cutting' or 'blunt' (almost the opposite of the prescribed meaning of 'precise'). So how far back do we go for an 'original' meaning? (Note once again that the teacher may well not be wrong in dissuading the child from using *nice* since it is inelegant to write 'It was a nice day so we went for a nice walk along a nice road . . .'. But this is poor style, not the use of a word with the 'wrong' meaning.)

Again, normative rules are based upon a particular, favoured form of the language. This may be the written form (we shall be discussing speech and writing in some detail later) or it may be the standard language, e.g. standard English. English that does not conform to this is 'sub-standard'. Grammatically, then, all of the following would be sub-standard:

> *They was there this morning.*
> *He ain't coming.*
> *Don't talk to I.*
> *I seed him this morning.*

Yet all of these are perfectly possible forms in some dialects of English. Why then are they 'ungrammatical'? The answer is quite simply that they are not standard English. There is no other answer to this question. The judgement, that is to say, is essentially a social one. People who speak like this do not belong to that branch of society that we recognize as educated. But it is most important to stress that in terms of linguistic efficiency these forms are no worse than those found in standard English. It is, moreover, largely a matter of historical accident whether one form rather than another has survived in this type of English. But surely, someone may object, *seed* is ungrammatical, because the past tense of *see* is *saw*? The answer is, of course, that *saw* is the past tense in standard English. But we can go no further. It is no good appealing to history since standard English too has abandoned many of its 'irregular' past tense forms in favour of forms ending in *-ed*. For instance, British English has *dived* where American also has *dove*. Standard English no less than the dialects has lost most of its inflections and there is no reason to argue that those that it has retained are somehow more valid grammatically, in any absolute sense. In many cases, moreover, we can actually invoke history on the side of the dialects rather than the standard language. Many English dialects, for instance, retain the *thou/ thee* forms with the corresponding forms of the verb. Yet forms like *dost*, *bist* (*beest*), as well as all the forms of the pronoun, would normally be regarded as sub-standard. But it would be reasonable to argue that the form of the language which retains these has a greater claim to respectability on grounds of linguistic history than a form which has lost the distinction between *thou/ thee* and *you*. Similarly, the form *'em* instead of *them* is usually considered to be uneducated. In actual fact it is not uncommon in the colloquial speech of perfectly well-educated people. There is no historical-linguistic reason to prefer *them*; on the contrary, the *'em* form is older – *them* is a comparatively recent intruder. It is, moreover, misleading to write *'em* with an apostrophe since it is not derived historically from *them* with the loss of its initial consonant; the [ð] (*th*) was never there.

It is wrong, then, to consider the dialect form as a corrupt form of the standard. Indeed it is always wrong to consider dialects as corrupt forms. They are not corrupt, but different, forms of the language. It may well be that they are not acceptable for many purposes, in the speech of educated people, in the mass media, etc., but this is wholly a matter of social convention, not of linguistic inferiority. This is in no way to deny the importance of social conventions. We break the conventions at our peril, we are dubbed 'ignorant', we fail to get the job we hoped for; but we ought not to provide pseudo-linguistic grounds to justify the conventions.

Finally in this section, it may be of interest to trace the origin of the normative rules. Most of them were invented by eighteenth-century grammarians and reinforced by their nineteenth- and even twentieth-century successors. One of the most notorious was Bishop Robert Lowth who in 1762 published *A Short Introduction to English Grammar*. He was in no doubt that the aim of his grammar was to show off 'every phrase and form of construction, whether it is right or not and . . . besides showing what is right . . . pointing out what is wrong'. Many of our normative rules are to be found in Lowth, though there is one at least that was not followed up – he advocated *sitten* instead of *sat*! The most famous, perhaps, of all grammars that followed Lowth is the *English Grammar* of 1795 by Lindlay Murray, in which grammar is defined as 'the Art of rightly expressing our thoughts by words'. Strangely enough it is with Murray and his contemporaries that we find English grammar no longer being described in terms of all the grammatical categories of Latin, a practice to be found in earlier grammars such as William Lily's *Short Introduction of Grammar* in the sixteenth century. But if the Latin categories were abandoned, the appeal to Latin for correctness was not. The rule concerning prepositions at the end of the sentence was taken up with fervour by the poet Dryden, who proceeded to 'correct' all his earlier works which contained this 'error'. Normative grammar is of course still with us, but the most notorious example within the last century is J. C. Nesfield's *Manual of English Grammar and Composition*, first published in 1898 and reprinted almost yearly after that and sold in huge quantities at home and abroad. Nesfield makes no major statements about the normative aims of grammar, but two of his sections are entitled *Purity of diction* and *Propriety of diction* and normative rules abound.

1.4 Speech and writing

We mentioned earlier the misconception, supported by the fact that the term 'grammar' comes from the Greek word meaning 'to write', that grammar is concerned with the written language. The Greek for 'grammar' is *grammatikē* or *grammatikē technē*, 'the art of writing'. This connotation remains in the term grammar school. From a descriptive point of view, however, there is no reason at all why we should restrict the term to the written language. Equally the spoken language has a grammar. Indeed there are still hundreds of languages in the world that have no written form yet they all have grammars in the sense in which we are interested in the term.

All too often people tend to think of the spoken language as a rather poor version of the written language. In pronunciation, for example, if someone is in doubt he is likely to appeal to the spelling. Often, in fact, in English the spelling is invoked against the normal usage. They will say 'Well, we pronounce it that way but really it is . . .'. I have heard this with the word *omelette*: 'We pronounce it "omelitte" [əmlit] but it is really "omelette" [əmlet]' (the square brackets indicate a phonetic transcription). We are all accustomed to the idea that English is not pronounced as it is spelt, yet so great is the authority of writing that we can provide a 'correct' pronunciation against the evidence of our own ears. Similarly, people will say that the word *ate* ought to be pronounced to rhyme with *gate* and that in this respect the Scottish pronunciation is correct and the English pronunciation incorrect. People write to the papers complaining about the pronunciation of Montgomery as 'Muntgummery'. They object, too, to the presence of *r* in *Shah of Persia* or the absence of an *r* in *far away* on the grounds that there is or is not an *r* in the spelling. Whether they are or are not right about the acceptability of such forms as standard English is another matter, but they should not argue the point on the grounds of spelling. Moreover, if the words are spelt differently, people will simply refuse to believe that they are pronounced in the same way. Many people (not all) make no distinction in speech between *mints* and *mince* or *patients* and *patience*, yet they will insist that they are different because the former of each pair 'has a *t* in it'. Greater incredulity or even hostility will meet the assertion that some well-educated people pronounce *tire* and *tower* like *tar*. Of course, not everyone does, nor even the majority of us; yet these pronunciations ARE to be found and may even be gaining ground. But there is no point in refusing to accept factual statements about this simply because it seems to be contrary to the evidence of the spelling.

A moment's reflection will soon make it clear that speech cannot in any serious sense be derived from writing and cannot therefore depend on it for correctness or non-correctness. Not only did the spoken language precede the written language historically (and even with a language like English only in very recent times has writing been at all widespread), but also every one of us learnt to speak long before we learnt to write. All the patterns of our language were quite firmly established before we went to school, and when we learnt to write we learnt only to put into written symbols what we already knew. If there is priority it is in the spoken, not the written form of language.

However, it may be objected that speech is ephemeral while writing is permanent, and that speech is full of errors and false starts while writing more correctly follows the rules. The first point is not, I think, relevant. It does not follow that speech has no grammar, just because, as soon as they are spoken, our words are lost for ever unless recorded on a tape recorder or other device. There is, however, an implication here that the written form carries the grammar because it, unlike speech, lasts over the centuries. Shakespeare's works for instance are still available today. But this argument would suggest that the grammar must always stay the same, that the grammar of Shakespeare is the same as the grammar of T. S. Eliot. To some degree this may be so, but it is no more obviously true (or false) of Shakespeare's and Eliot's writing than it is of Shakespeare's and Eliot's speech. The only difference is that because the written records survive we are in a position to compare their written texts but not their speech. It is also true that the written language changes more slowly than the spoken and that it is therefore always more archaic, but this too is not an argument for the suggestion that it and it alone contains the grammar. There is yet a further point: the written language is often far more homogeneous than the spoken. Because it is the language of education it tends to be the same all over the country, whereas the spoken language differs and is represented by many dialects. But this is equally irrelevant. All it could possibly imply would be that there was only one grammar for the whole of say, the written English language for 300 years over the whole of Britain and the USA, but a lot of different grammars for the spoken language. I do not in fact believe this would be a fair statement of the facts, but even if it were, it would not seriously suggest that grammar was to be found only in the written language.

In many ways, moreover, the written language is a far worse

vehicle of communication than the spoken. If we take the number of letters of the alphabet used for English we find they are insufficient to represent all the possible pronunciations (if we decided to reform the spelling, we should have to invent some new symbols). For instance, English has six 'short' or 'non-final' vowels (i.e. vowel sounds that do not occur at the end of words), but only five vowel symbols *a*, *e*, *i*, *o*, and *u*. What happens then when we have a contrast of all six? If we look at English monosyllabic words we can find only two sets of words with all six possibilities:

pit	*rick*
pet	*wreck*
pat	*rack, wrack*
pot	*rock*
putt	*ruck*
put	*rook*

Of particular interest are the devices used to distinguish the last two of each of the set. In the first we write a double *t* for *putt*; in the second we use the symbol *oo* for *rook*.

Much more striking is the failure of the written language to carry much of English intonation. If for instance I say *She's very pretty* with a final rising or falling intonation I make a bald statement, but if I use a falling-rising intonation on the last word, I am saying 'She's very pretty, but . . .', leaving it to my hearer to infer what reservations I have. This cannot be represented at all in the written language. Yet it is an essential part of the language and even, perhaps, of the grammar. We may compare the use of a rising intonation for *She's pretty?* and the alternative *Is she pretty?* In the second of these there is a grammatical device that changes the order of the words to form the question. The intonation has a similar function, but it is a moot point whether this too should be regarded as a matter of grammar. Certainly we cannot deal with this here.

Intonation can, of course, mark grammatical distinctions that are also marked by punctuation. There is a difference in intonation between such phrases as

She speaks French, naturally.
She speaks French naturally.
My brother, who is in London
My brother who is in London
Do you like coffee, or tea?
Do you like coffee or tea?

This shows that intonation is often a mark of a grammatical distinction that is made in writing. But we do not have to conclude that grammatical distinctions rest solely upon the written form. Precisely what the distinctions are and how we account for them is a different and difficult matter, but they are just as relevant for speech as for writing, and are often to be found in speech alone.

There are many differences between a spoken and a written language. Some are obvious and some are due directly to the difference of the media of sounds versus symbols. I do not intend to discuss here such notorious misfits as *-ough* in *cough, tough, though, bough, through, thought* and *thorough*. But let us look instead at some grammatical differences. We cannot consider syntax in any detail, as it is by no means easy to show any clear-cut differences, but there is one example which is interesting. In written English we would normally wish to avoid *I only saw John* because we do not know whether it means 'All I did was to see John' or 'John was the only one I saw.' Moreover, we should usually be told that the sentence could not have the second of these two meanings; for that, we ought to write *I saw John only*. But none of these considerations is at all valid for spoken English. There is no ambiguity since the intonation shows quite clearly whether we mean *only saw* or *only . . . John*. In the written language there are reasons for arguing that *only* should be placed next to the word it modified; in the spoken language there are no such reasons, because the intonation clearly indicates with which it is to be linked.

Turning to morphological (inflectional) characteristics we find quite striking differences between the spoken and the written language. In the English number system, for example, there are three common ways of deriving plurals from singulars:

(1) add -*s*   *cat, cats*
(2) 'zero' ending   *sheep, sheep*
(3) change the vowel *mouse, mice*

All three plurals are found in the spoken language; in fact the same words would be examples. But there are some words which belong to different types in the two forms of the language. For instance in the written language *postman/postmen* belongs to (3) along with *mouse/mice*. In speech, however, it belongs to (2) with *sheep/sheep* since the spoken form is identical in both cases. If we *say*

> *The postman came up the street.*

there is nothing to show that it is different from

> *The postmen came up the street.*

How many postmen? One or more than one? We do not know; the form is the same, phonetically [pousmən], in both cases. Of course we CAN provide a pronunciation that makes the difference, a 'spelling' pronunciation; but such a pronunciation is an artificial one used only when there is pressure to resolve ambiguity. To point to this when discussing the spoken form is cheating – it is assuming that the speech must reflect the writing, and with that assumption, of course, the spoken language cannot have a different grammar.

Another example is to be found in the plural of *house*. In the written language it is regular – *houses*. But in speech it is irregular since the last consonant phonetically [s] is replaced by [z] before the added ending. It is [hauziz] and not [hausiz]. No other word in the English language is exactly parallel; other words with a final [s] do not replace it with [z] in the plural, e.g. *face, horse, lease, moose*, etc. (If in fact we had a similar plural for *face, faces* would be pronounced exactly as *phases*.) All these then retain the [s] in the plural while *house* has a change to [z]. The nearest feature similar to this is found in *wife/wives, knife/knives, wreath/wreaths*, etc., all of which involve changing a voiceless final consonant (one made without vibration of the vocal cords) in the singular for a voiced consonant (one made with vibration of the vocal cords) in the plural, [f] vs. [v] and [θ] vs. [ð]. The [s]/[z] contrast is similarly one of voiceless and voiced consonants, but this particular contrast is otherwise unknown for the singular/ plural relation. Note that the writing DOES indicate the difference between *f* and *v* in the examples quoted, but it does not always do so, for instance in many people's pronunciation of *roofs* (which could have been, but is not, written as **rooves*). But the *th* distinction as in *wreath/wreaths* is never made because English has only one way of representing these two different sounds.

There are other examples in the English verb. There is nothing irregular about *does* in the written form. It is exactly parallel with *goes* – *do/does*, *go/goes*. But in speech the form is quite irregular – it is [dʌz]. We find in fact that the auxiliary verbs of English, BE, WILL, SHALL, CAN, MUST, etc., have plenty of irregular forms, though not all of them are irregular in the written form. Thus the negative *won't*, *shan't*, *can't* are irregularly formed from *will*, *shall* and *can*, but there is nothing irregular about *mustn't*. But in speech it IS irregular since t is omitted in the negative – [mʌsnt] not **[mʌstnt]. Most of the auxiliary verbs have irregular *-s* forms ('third person singular') in both speech and writing – *is*, *has*, *does*, *can* (not **cans*), *will* (not **wills*), etc. There is just one verb in English that has an irregular *-s* form, yet is never an auxiliary but always a main verb. I have asked English people many times to tell me which one this is and seldom do I get an answer, so ignorant are we all of the grammar of our own language. The answer is the verb SAY whose *-s* form *says* is [sez] and not [seiz]. Strangely enough comic writers use the form *sez* as in '*Sez 'e*' to indicate a sub-standard form, yet it is a fair representation of a completely normal standard form.

In French we find considerable differences in the forms of written and spoken languages. A striking example is to be found in the feminine forms of the adjectives. The rule in the written language is to add an *-e* to form the feminine. In the spoken form the difference consists of the presence of a consonant in the feminine that is absent in the masculine:

vert	*verte*	vɛr	vɛrt	green
grand	*grande*	grã	grãd	big
gris	*grise*	gri	griz	grey
long	*longue*	lõ	lõg	long

It might at first seem necessary to say that a consonant is added to the masculine to form the feminine. But the consonant that is added varies from word to word. There is a much better solution: the masculine is formed from the feminine by deleting the final consonant. This may seem a novel way of treating these forms, but it is clearly the simplest.

In these examples there is at least parallelism. We add an *-e* to the feminine in the written and delete the final consonant in the masculine in the spoken. But for other words the two systems are quite 'out of phase'. Sometimes the writing makes a distinction that the spoken form does not:

fier	*fière*	fjɛr	fjɛr	proud
grec	*grecque*	grɛk	grɛk	Greek

Sometimes the spoken form has a different consonant:

neuf	*neuve*	nœf	nœv	new

and so on.

Of course, people will try to explain the spoken form in terms of the written, and say for instance that 'the final *e* shows that the consonant must be pronounced'. But this is nonsense except as a hint about the way to read written French. In the spoken form there IS NO final consonant except in the feminine. It is always pronounced when it is there, and if it is not there, as in the masculine, it is neither pronounced nor 'silent'! Moreover, how could such a statement be true of a native French speaker? He knew how to form the masculine and feminine forms of the adjective BEFORE he learnt to write them down. It would make nonsense, therefore, to account for the spoken grammar in terms of the written. The reverse might be possible, but even that is misleading. They are two different grammars, though they have many parallel features.

One moral that might be drawn from all this is that English and French would be better languages if they reformed their writing to correspond with speech. But from the point of view of grammar this would be most unfortunate, for the written grammar is in many respects simpler than the spoken (not always – the French verb has far too many endings). For instance, the French device of an *-e* for the feminine ending is simpler than the spoken device of deleting the final consonant, because a deleted consonant cannot be 'recovered'. That is to say if we hear the masculine form we cannot predict the feminine (though this does not really matter for the Frenchman, who knows them both very well). But in the writing we can predict, often at least, both from feminine to masculine and vice versa. Another example comes from English. In the written language we form *photography* and *photographic* from *photograph* by adding endings. In speech we change the whole of the vowel system – [fətəgrəfi, foutəgræfik, foutəgrɑːf]. The writing again is more convenient; it indicates a 'base' form that does not really exist in the speech, though we might, as grammarians, reconstruct it. Often in this way writing clarifies important grammatical features of the speech. This might be an additional reason for thinking that writing is 'more grammatical'. But the truth of this depends on what is meant by 'grammatical'. Writing is 'more grammatical' in the sense that it often indicates grammatical relationships more clearly, as in the example quoted. It does not, of course, follow that it is 'more grammatical' in the sense of being more correct.

1.5 Form and meaning

Another of the misconceptions that we discussed is that grammar is essentially concerned with meaning. In linguistics, however, we draw a distinction between grammar and semantics (the study of meaning) and insist that they are not identified.

It is easy enough to show that grammatical distinctions are not semantic ones by indicating the many cases where there is not a one-to-one correspondence. An often quoted example is that of *oats* and *wheat*. The former is clearly plural and the latter singular. This is partly indicated by the ending -*s* (though this is not an unambiguous sign of the plural in view of a word like *news* which is singular) but is clearly shown by the fact that we say *The oats are* . . ., *The wheat is* . . . We cannot, however, say in all seriousness that *oats* are 'more than one' while *wheat* is 'one', though these are the traditional definitions of singular and plural. Some people might say that this is true of English, but that is only to say that *oats* is GRAMMATICALLY plural and *wheat* GRAMMATICALLY singular. If these people go on to insist, as some do, that the English think of *oats* as plural and of *wheat* as singular, then this has to be rejected as simply false. There is then no clear one-to-one relation between the grammatical categories of singular and plural and counting in terms of 'one' and 'more than one'. Further examples are to be found in *foliage* vs *leaves*, in English *hair* which is singular vs French *cheveux*, plural. These distinctions are grammatical and do not directly correspond to any categories of meaning. An old joke emphasizes this point:

TEACHER: Is 'trousers' singular or plural?
JOHNNY: Please, Sir, singular at the top and plural at the bottom.

The same kind of considerations hold for sex and gender. The Romance languages, especially French, provide examples of this. First, in these languages every noun is either masculine or feminine, e.g. French *le livre* (masculine) 'the book', *la porte* (feminine) 'the door'. Similarly in Italian we find *il libro*, *la porta*, Spanish *el libro*, *la puerta*. The similarity of these forms with their genders is a result of their common relationship with the 'parent' language Latin (though Latin has a third gender, neuter). It would make nonsense, however, to say that French, Italian and Spanish people think of all objects as male or female. They do not; it is simply that the grammar of their language divides all nouns into two classes. The essential characteristics of the classification is that members of each class are accompanied by different forms of their article, and of adjectives – *le livre vert*, *la porte verte* 'the green book', 'the green door'. The irrelevance of any kind of meaning to gender is further illustrated by comparing the genders of words in one language with those in another. A well-known comparison is the gender of the words for 'sun' and 'moon' in the Romance languages and in German. In the Romance languages 'sun' is masculine and 'moon' feminine (French *le soleil*, *la lune*, Italian *il sole*, *la luna*, Spanish *el sol*, *la luna*), but in German 'sun' is feminine and 'moon' masculine (*die Sonne*, *der Mond*).

A second point is that there are plenty of nouns which, though feminine, normally refer to men, e.g. French *la sentinelle* 'the sentinel', *la vigi* 'the night watchman', *la recru* 'the recruit'. Indeed, most of these names of occupation are feminine even though the person referred to is often a strapping young man. In German there is an even more striking situation. German has three genders – masculine, feminine AND neuter – *der Tisch* (masculine) 'the table', *die Tür* (feminine) 'the door', *das Feuer* (neuter) 'the fire', but the two words commonly used to refer to girls and young ladies are neuter – *das Mädchen* and *das Fräulein*! Mark Twain makes use of this confusion of gender and sex in his *A Tramp Abroad*:

GRETCHEN: Wilhelm, where is the turnip?
WILHELM: She has gone to the kitchen.
GRETCHEN: Where is the accomplished and beautiful English maiden?
WILHELM: It has gone to the opera.

Thirdly, adjectives indicating sex often occur with nouns of the 'opposite' gender. In French, 'the mouse' is *la souris* and 'the he-mouse' is *la souris mâle* – 'the male (feminine) mouse'! In Latin, similarly, though *lupus* (masculine) is 'a wolf', the feminine *lupa* is not usually 'she-wolf'. 'She-wolf' is *lupus femina*, while *lupa* is 'a prostitute'. But there is nothing odd about this provided we do not identify grammatical gender with biological sex.

It is not true, of course, that gender has nothing at all to do with sex in the European languages. There is a link, but a tenuous one. For most creatures that are obviously male or female the words will normally be masculine and feminine respectively. Thus *l'homme* 'the man' is masculine and *la femme* 'the woman' is feminine (cf. Italian *il uomo*, *la donna*, Spanish *el hombre*, *la mujer*).

In English there is no gender in this sense at all, no grammatical gender. We have words that refer to male and female creatures – *bull/cow*, *ram/ewe*, *boar/sow* etc. but this is not a matter of grammar and should be dealt with in the lexicon or dictionary. If we want to include this in grammar we ought also to find a place there for the names of the baby creatures – *calf*, *lamb*, *piglet* – for the language makes distinction between young and adult in just the same way as it does between male and female, and there is no obvious reason why the one should be thought grammatical but not the other. The traditional grammarians have dealt only with sex distinctions, but the reason is all too obvious: gender is assumed to be a characteristic of all languages because of Latin and is therefore assumed to be a category of English, but there is no evidence for grammatical distinctions in terms of size. There are also some words in English which differ in form in terms of a sex relationship, especially in the ending *–ess*: *author*, *authoress*; *tiger*, *tigress*; *duke*, *duchess*. Is this not perhaps gender? The answer again must be 'no'. It is not enough to have different endings for the pair of words, they must also involve grammatical features of a syntactic nature, restrictional features (see p. 98). In the Romance languages, gender determines the form of the article and the adjectives, but there is no similar feature in English. If endings alone were sufficient, then again we ought to ask for a similar treatment for *pig/piglet*; *duck/duckling*; *goose/gosling*. This is a noteworthy feature of the English language but it is NOT gender.

Yet, no doubt, someone will still insist that English has gender; what about *he/she/it*, *him/her/it*, *his/her/its*? The answer is that these ARE used for sex reference, and for precisely this reason there is no need to talk about gender. Not only do we say

> *The man has left his food,*
> *The woman has left her food,*

but also

> *The cat has left his food,*
> *The cat has left her food,*

according to whether we are talking about a tom-cat or a she-cat.

The choice of the pronoun, that is to say, depends directly on the sex of the creature referred to, and there is, therefore, nothing more that has to be said in the grammar. A further point is that the noun/pronoun relation does not often involve a clearly stateable restriction – we can say *The girl lost her hat* or *The girl lost his hat*. The choice depends on the meaning. With *himself* or *herself*, however, there are strict restrictions – *The girl washed herself*, not ... *himself* – and here alone we might seem to be within the province of grammar. Ships are, of course, referred to as *she* and so often are cars, at least by men. We should not build a grammatical theory around this rather special case. It is enough to say that the Englishman treats them as if they were female; we can then provide the joking explanation – that they are fickle, stubborn, etc.

It is interesting to note, furthermore, that the close relationship between grammar and sex is largely restricted to languages with which scholars are most familiar, those of the Indo-European and Semitic groups. In other languages, especially in Africa, gender in a strict grammatical sense has nothing to do with sex, but is concerned with the distinction between living and non-living creatures and even between big and small (see p. 87).

Less obvious than the distinction between gender and sex is that between tense and time. Most European languages have special forms of the verb to mark tense – past, present and future. But it would be a mistake to think in terms of some universal characteristic of time markers in the verb. In English the position is rather complex and will therefore be discussed later when we deal in detail with English tense (pp. 193–6), but two points may be made here. First, if the English past tense refers to past time why do we say

> *If I knew, I would tell you,*

or   *I wish I knew*?

The form *knew* is the past tense form of the verb *know*, cf. *I know it now* and *I knew it all yesterday*. But we use the past tense forms of the verb in the two constructions illustrated above, cf. also *if I loved, if I went, I wish I had*, etc. There is an escape: we say these are not really past tense forms – they are subjunctives or something like that. But this is cheating. It is like pretending that stealing is not a crime by calling it borrowing, a pure terminological trick. The simple fact is that the past tense form does not always refer to past time. Secondly, if we recognize tense wherever we have time relations, why not talk about tense in the noun too? It has been suggested that in that case *fiancée* is future tense, *ex-wife* past tense and *grandfather* pluperfect!

Finally, in this section, we should look at the traditional approach to the definition of the parts of speech, since it too is partly at least in notional terms. For instance, Nesfield defines a noun as 'A word used for naming anything' and notes that 'thing' in the definition stands for person, place, quality, action, feeling, collection, etc.! This is clearly a notional definition at its worst. For how do we know what a thing is? Is fire a thing? Is peace? Is hope or intention? Moreover, can we not say that *red* is the name of a colour and is not *red* then a noun? Nesfield talks about qualities as things but one would normally think that the words for qualities were adjectives – *brave, foolish, good*, etc. In fact the definition is completely vacuous as we can see if we ask how on the basis of this definition can we find the nouns in *He suffered terribly* and *His suffering was terrible*? Is there any sense in which the last sentence has reference to things in a way in which the first does not? For these sentences are identical in meaning. Of course we can say that 'suffering' is a noun and that in this sentence it refers to a thing, the act of suffering being 'treated' as a thing, but this is arguing back to front.

How can we possibly identify 'thing'? There is an easy answer. We do so by using an article or such words as *his, this,* in front of the words – *the fire, the suffering, the place* – and by making them the subject of the sentence. But this is to say that we identify 'things' by looking for the grammatical characteristics of nouns. In other words 'things' are identified by being referred to by nouns. A definition, then, of nouns in terms of things is completely circular. There is no confusion of semantics and grammar this time, merely a failure to recognize that there is no clearly identifiable independent criterion of 'thing'.

The whole of this section is aimed at showing that grammatical categories must be grammatical and not semantic. But we must not overstate the case. There are two reservations to be made. First, we shall often find correlation between grammatical and semantic categories, e.g. between gender and sex, number and counting. This is not surprising, for grammar has a job to do; it would be more surprising if it bore no relation at all to our every-day needs and experience. But it should not be identified with semantics, and we need not expect any one-to-one correlation. Secondly, as linguists we must write our grammars in such a way that they relate to semantics as well as to phonetics – our grammar must be 'sensitive' to semantics. This needs to be said because there was once a strong school of thought that advocated 'formal grammar' (see p. 110), i.e. grammar that is based exclusively on (phonetic and phonological) form. This was far too extreme a requirement. It turned out to be quite unworkable in any case; no one ever succeeded in writing a grammar that paid no attention at all to features of meaning. Moreover, would we want such a grammar? Is not the whole purpose of describing a language to relate sounds to meaning? Formal grammar was certainly useful, however, as a reaction against older, notional views of grammar.

2. Some traditional concepts

Traditional grammars make use of a fairly wide technical vocabulary to describe the concepts they use – words like 'noun', 'verb', 'agreement', 'plural', 'clause' and even 'word' itself. Some of the terms are probably unintelligible to most people, though they may have some dim recollection of them from their schooldays. Others would be more familiar – most people would know, or think they know, what is meant by 'plural' or 'noun' and everyone, I suspect, would be convinced that he knew what a word was. However, we cannot take even this for granted. We must look at both the familiar and the less familiar terms to see precisely how they are used and to ask whether their use is really justified. Unfortunately the usual practice in the grammar is to give some kind of definition of most of the words, but never to question the whole justification of their use.

In this chapter I shall first explain how some of the more important terms have been used in the past, but secondly, and more importantly, discuss the value of some of the concepts and the ways in which they can be or have been used in more recent studies of linguistics.

2.1 Words

In literate societies, at least, the word is so much a part of everyday knowledge that it is completely taken for granted. Grammar books often make no attempt to give a definition of the word though they happily define other grammatical elements in terms of it. The sentence, for instance, is a 'combination of words' and the parts of speech are 'classes of words'. But what a word is and how it can be defined is often not considered.

The chief reason for this is that in the written language there is no doubt at all about the status of the word. Words are clearly identified by the spaces between them. On any page of print we can simply count how many words there are by counting the groups of letters that are separated by spaces. Moreover, with one or two exceptions, which are mostly concerned with hyphens, everyone knows just where to put the spaces. (Exceptions are of the kind *well-chosen* or *well chosen* or perhaps even *wellchosen*.) The word is part of our writing conventions and we learn what words are when we first learn to spell. The placing of the spaces is as much a part of our education and is as well established as spelling and punctuation, perhaps more so than the latter.

However, we are not concerned only with writing, but also with speech. Are there, similarly, words in the spoken language? It is not easy to give a direct answer to this question. There are three points that we should consider.

First, we must not simply project the written word on to the spoken word. That is, we must not assume that wherever we have words in writing we must have words in speech. This is a clear example of one of the areas in language study in which we must keep speech and writing distinct, even if it is very difficult to do so. After an education that has been largely in terms of the written word the average person finds it very difficult to question the universally held assumption that there are words in the spoken language too. But if we are to look at language objectively we must question this assumption.

Secondly, it is a fact that there are no spaces between 'words' in speech. This comes as a surprise to many people. So great is the influence of writing that they actually 'hear' in speech what they see in writing. Even some grammarians have made this mistake. They have been misled by a false parallelism between speech and writing and have assumed that there are slight pauses between words. This point can be proved quite easily by carefully listening to people speaking – there are no breaks between the 'words'. What breaks there are, come at the end of groups of 'words' – phrases, clauses, sentences. This is borne out, too, by experimental phonetics. Any kind of visual representation of speech by mechanical or electronic instruments (and there are many kinds) show speech as a continuum without any breaks at the points where the written words would be divided. More convincingly, perhaps, if we listen to an unfamiliar language we find it quite impossible to divide up the speech into any kind of limited stretches except those marked by pauses and by intonation, but these are always very much larger than single words. Clearly, recognizing the word in speech is not a matter of detecting breaks in the stream of speech, for there are no breaks to detect. There are, however, as we shall see later in this chapter, some features that mark off stretches of speech that partially at least (and in different ways in different languages) correspond to the words of the written language.

Thirdly, it is highly probable that the words of the written language are not purely conventional. They more likely correspond to some kind of linguistically justified unit. That is, we should expect to find that there are some principles underlying word division. It would otherwise be extremely difficult for the child to learn the rules for written word division and even highly educated adults could be expected to make far more mistakes than they actually do. Moreover, it is said that even in nonliterate societies there is a clear recognition of the word – that the word is 'institutionalized'. I am not sure that this is very significant, for its relevance will depend on what is meant by 'clear recognition'. It may well mean no more than that linguists are able on the basis of the linguistic behaviour of these people to establish the words of the language (by methods of the kind we shall soon be considering). It is all too easy to see as linguistic realities those linguistic entities that we wish to establish in order to undertake our description of the language. There is, furthermore, some quite good evidence that the word is NOT a natural linguistic entity. We have only to look at ancient inscriptions to see this. The use of space to indicate word division belongs to Roman times; the Greeks did not use spaces, but ran all their words together. But even here we would be on dangerous ground if we said the Greeks had no notion of the word, for the whole of one work of the Greek philosopher Plato, the *Cratylus*, is about language, and is largely centred upon items that are unmistakably words.

We have to ask ourselves, then, quite objectively, what a word is, how it can be defined and even perhaps whether there are words in the spoken language. There have been three main approaches to this problem. The first is to see the word as a semantic unit, a unit of meaning; the second sees it as a phonetic or phonological unit, one that is marked, if not by 'spaces' or pauses, at least by some features of the sounds of the language; the third attempts to establish the word by a variety of linguistic procedures that are associated with the idea that the word is in some ways an isolable and indivisible unit.

Let us begin by looking at semantic definitions of the word. In fact these are not so much semantic as notional, and fail for all the reasons we have already discussed in dealing with form and meaning. The word is said to be a linguistic unit that has a single meaning. The difficulty, of course, is in deciding what is meant by a single meaning, for meanings are no more easily identified than words. It is easy enough to show in a variety of ways that we cannot define words in terms of units of meaning. To begin with, it is very clear that very many single words cover not one but two or more 'bits' of meaning. If *sing* has a single meaning, then presumably *singer* has more since it means *one who sings* and even *sang* must mean both *sing* and 'past time'. Similarly we can hardly say that *lamb*, *ewe* and *ram* have single meanings since they all mean 'sheep' but 'baby', 'mother' and 'father' as well. It is, moreover, a pure accident whether we use one or two words to describe the baby, the female or the male of any species. Alongside *lamb*, *ewe* and *ram* we have *elephant calf*, *elephant cow* and *elephant bull*. The reason for the difference is obvious – we are less familiar in our culture (or at least our ancestors were less familiar) with elephants than with sheep – but that proves nothing about the amount of meaning in one word. Even with objects that are more familiar to modern society there are similar discrepancies. We have to use two words to distinguish *passenger train* from *goods train*, though for a similar distinction with road vehicles we have *bus* and *lorry*. The point is stressed even further if we look at other languages. The Eskimo has three words for different kinds of snow, the Bedouin has many words for all the different kinds of camel that he recognizes. To translate these into English we have to use more than a single word. But what does this prove about meaning? Nothing more than that single words do not appear to have single meanings, even if we could (which I doubt) establish single meanings. Conversely there are combinations of words in English that do not have separate meanings. *Put up with*, for instance, cannot be divided into the three meaning units of *put*, *up* and *with*, but seems to have the single meaning of 'tolerate'. There are dozens of combinations of this kind in English, mostly of two words – *make up, take to, look for, put off, take in*, etc. These are all idioms, of course, but the whole point about idioms is that they cannot be divided into separate units of meaning.

Yet a further point about the relation of word to meaning arises from the fact that very often word division does not appear to correspond to meaning division. For instance, we cannot divide *heavy smoker* into *heavy* and *smoker* if we are thinking in terms of meaning, for a *heavy smoker* is not both a smoker and heavy. Another example quoted in some text books to make this point is *artificial florist* (one who sells artificial flowers). More striking, perhaps, is *criminal lawyer* who is not both *criminal* and *lawyer*. In all these examples the main meaning division does not correspond to the word division. Rather we should place it within the second word – *heavy smok/er, artificial flor/ist, criminal law/yer*. An even more difficult example (it is a notorious one in linguistic discussion and will turn up again later) is *the King of England's hat*. If we try to link meanings to words we shall have to give a meaning to *England's* (or at best associate closely the meanings, if more than one, of *England's*). Yet is it quite clear that *England's* is no kind of unit at all – the *'s* that shows possession does not go with *England* but with *the King of England*. Clearly as far as meaning is concerned the word is not a single unit, nor is it even a close-knit group of related units of meaning. Indeed, any attempt to define the word in terms of a unit of meaning will be circular; we shall ultimately have to define 'unit of meaning' in terms of the word.

This is even true of words which appear to stand for objects, for, as we have seen, a single object may well be designated by one or more words, and 'designating a single object' can hardly be regarded as the same as 'having a single meaning'. Otherwise we should have to say that 'a clever little English boy with fair hair, blue eyes and a mischievous smile' represents a unit of meaning. It would not be utterly unreasonable, moreover, to suppose that our language might have designated such an object with a single word!

What about the phonetic and phonological definitions of the word? In some languages it is indeed quite possible to recognize a word by some feature of its pronunciation. There are some languages, for instance, which have what is known as 'fixed stress': the stress always falls on one particular syllable of the word, not as in English or Russian where it falls on different syllables in different words. It always falls in these languages on the first syllable or the last or the last but one and so on; sometimes it is a little more complex than this but still 'fixed' and predictable. Clearly by simply counting forward or backwards we can establish where the word begins or ends and can thereby divide up any stretch of speech into words. A slightly more 'exotic' feature that is found in many languages is 'vowel harmony' which is often but not always a characteristic of the word. In such languages all the vowels of any one word have a particular quality and it is quite clear therefore that if we recognize a change in the quality of the vowel we know that there is word division. Vowel harmony is found in many languages – Turkish, Hungarian, Somali, Tigre (Ethiopia), Igbo (Nigeria) – though it is not always a feature of whole words. Sometimes the vowels are of a more open or close quality, sometimes more front and back, sometimes rounded or unrounded (open and close, front and back refer to the position of the tongue, round and unrounded to the position of the lips). An excellent example is Turkish; in the following examples the vowels are all either front or back and rounded or unrounded within the word:

ev	house	*evim*	my house (front, unrounded)
göz	eye	*gözüm*	my eye (front, rounded)
yol	way	*yolum*	my way (back, rounded)
kız	daughter	*kızım*	my daughter (back, unrounded).

English has nothing quite like this, but there are two features that are associated with the word. The first is stress; what we may call 'full' stress, though not placed on any particular syllable, nevertheless falls on only one syllable in each word. By this means we can argue that even if we ignore our writing conventions *blackbird*, *blackboard*, *greenhouse*, etc. are single words as compared with *black bird*, *black board*, *green house*. Unfortunately there is not a really consistent relationship between stress patterns and our writing conventions. *The White House*, for instance, is pronounced as if *White House* were one word (compare *the white house*), but is not written as one. It is a very common device in English to link two nouns by the use of a single stress but there is no consistency about the writing of them as one or two words. Alongside *table top*, *cushion cover*, *bread shop*, *shoe polish* we find *inkwell*, *beehive*, *cowshed*, *birdcage* (or with hyphens only). More striking, perhaps, and more important is the fact that many of the little words that have a grammatical function rather than a lexical one (i.e. that are not likely to be treated in detail in the dictionary) are often unstressed and seem to belong to the stress pattern of a preceding or following word. Thus *beat her* is often pronounced in exactly the same way as *beater* and *kissed her* rhymes with *sister* as we well know from 'O my Darling Clementine'. Some linguists have, indeed, regarded these as 'phonological' words.

English also has what is commonly known as 'juncture'. This is illustrated by the fact that even in normal speech it is possible to distinguish between

that stuff	*that's tough*
a nice cake	*an ice cake*
keep sticking	*keeps ticking*
grey day	*Grade A*

The vowels and consonants of each pair are identical. How, then, do they differ? They are said to differ in juncture. The precise signal for this distinction varies – in the case of the third pair the noticeable feature is the aspiration (the 'h'-like sound) that follows the articulation of the *t* of *ticking*, and elsewhere it is largely a matter of the timing of the various articulatory movements. What is important here is not the precise phonetics, but the fact that it is clear that we CAN distinguish the pairs. We have, it follows, marks of word division since we can distinguish between two utterances that are otherwise identical; the difference must surely be related to the fact that the word division is different. Unfortunately this will not always work. There is no distinction at all in normal speech between *a tack* and *attack*, yet these two are quite different from the first two syllables of *at Acton*. Here the juncture allows us to distinguish between two sequences of words that are divided differently, but not between the first of these sequences and the single word. Similarly in *the potato* there is no way of showing that the division is between *the* and *potato* rather than between *the po-* and *-tato* though we do know it is NOT between *the pot-* and *-ato* for exactly the same reasons as those that allow us to distinguish *attack* and *a tack* from *at Acton*. One linguist actually marked juncture within the word *potato* and so treated *potato* as two 'words' because of this fact, but clearly his junctures do not correspond to word division as we know it. It has been pointed out moreover that in most people's speech *at all* is pronounced as if it were *a tall* – in other words the juncture feature suggests the WRONG word division. The reason here is that *at all* is treated by most of us as if it were a single word like *nearly, wholly*, etc.; as a single word it would be phonetically identical with **atall*, just as there is no difference between *attack* and *a tack*. So it is not really an exception.

The real difficulties about using juncture as a means of establishing word divisions are:

(1) that the features are not always present – whether we can distinguish between *that's tough* and *that stuff* depends on a variety of factors including the speed of utterance, and the dis-

tinction can be guaranteed a reasonable degree of success only in very careful utterances;

(2) that juncture features mark only some word divisions – they do not, for instance, as we have seen, distinguish *a tack* and *attack*.

We must ask, however, quite seriously, whether all this is really relevant. Even if we had clear features of sound marking off words would they then define words or should we look elsewhere for the definition? Is it not perhaps the case that phonetic definitions of the word are as irrelevant as semantic ones – that the word ought to be definable as some kind of clearly establishable GRAMMATICAL unit? We may be thankful that we have clues to word division, but the clues are only clues and not part of the criteria. This leads on to the third kind of approach (see p. 44) to the definition of the word. A simple and plausible definition is in terms not of pause, but of POTENTIAL pause. We can establish words by asking where we can pause if we so wish. So we know that there are three words *I saw John* because we can divide by pausing, into *I* and *saw John*, and *I saw* and *John*. But this is unsatisfactory because we almost certainly pause where we 'know' there are words in the sense of knowing where the spaces would come in the writing. This then merely takes over the written word by allowing potential pause wherever there are spaces. Moreover is it really true that we can only pause between words? Surely we can pause in deliberate speech between the parts of *postman*, *sleepless* and even *discuss* and *consider*. This may perhaps suggest that these are TWO words in speech, but do we want to say that? We can even invent situations in which we can divide speech into syllables or even into letter-sounds. *c - a - t*. Do these then become words? It depends obviously on what is meant by 'potential' in the phrase 'potential pause'.

There are similar difficulties with any definition of the word as an 'indivisible unit'. It is sometimes suggested, for instance, that a word is a linguistic unit which does not permit the insertion of any other linguistic material. For instance, we know that *little boy* is two words because we can insert *English* – *little English boy* – but we cannot insert anything within, say, *singing*. But this too turns out to be false for we can divide singing into two parts, *sing-* and *-ing*, and insert *-ing and danc-* to give us *singing and dancing*. Of course we did not insert a word or even whole words, but that is no objection. If we have not yet established what a word is we cannot require that the 'no insertion' criterion applies only to complete words!

A famous definition of the word in linguistic circles that suffers from the same defects is that of the great American linguist Leonard Bloomfield. He defined a word as a 'minimum free form'. What he meant was the smallest bit of speech that can occur in isolation. But again what we are prepared to utter in isolation is almost certainly what we have learnt to recognize as a word in writing. Certainly many 'words' would not occur by themselves in any natural conversation. We should find it difficult to provide a context for the occurrence in isolation of *the* or *a* or *my* and in French of *à* or *je*, except one in which we were deliberately talking about words, e.g. 'What is the first word in *the book*?' or even the apparently harmless 'What comes before *book* in *the book*?' It is obvious, however, that questions like this, questions ABOUT language, cannot fairly be used to establish what words are. First, they assume again that we already know what words are, and secondly we could produce quite bogus words by asking for instance 'What comes before *-ject* in *reject*?' (answer '*re*'), or 'What is the last element of *boy's*?' (answer '*s*'), or 'What have *pity* and *intensity* in common?' (answer '*ity*'). In other words, anything can occur in isolation if we want to talk about it. If Bloomfield's test is to be of any use we must restrict our attention to ordinary language and not to language about language. One way out of the difficulty that has been proposed is to say that words like *the, a, my, je*, etc., while not themselves minimum free forms, nevertheless function in essentially the same way as many others that are. *The*, for instance, and *a* are like *this* and *that*, which do occur alone, and French *je* is like *Pierre*. But this does not help, since the English possessive *'s* as in *John's* is like *of*, and the prefix *in-* in *intolerable* is like *not*, but this would not be a good argument for treating them as

words. (There is a story about the film producer Sam Goldwyn –
a 'Goldwynism' – in which he allegedly said 'I can describe
your proposal in just two words – "Im possible!"') Moreover,
some of these forms are quite clearly forms that are not used in
isolation because the language has a different form for use in
isolation. We have no form in isolation to correspond to *the* and
a, but we do have *mine* and *yours* for *my* and *your*, and French
moi for *je* and *lui* for *il*. The evidence for these forms suggests,
in fact, that the forms that are never used in isolation are NOT
minimum free forms.

In conclusion, sadly, we have to say that the word is not a
clearly definable linguistic unit. We shall, perhaps, have to
recognize some kind of unit that corresponds closely to the written word and define it ultimately in terms of a combination of the
features we have been considering, though as we shall see in the
next chapter some theorists have decided to do without the word
altogether. But what the word is or is not depends ultimately on
our TOTAL view of grammar.

2.2 Inflection and syntax

We saw in the last section that traditional grammars treat words
as their basic units. There is, however, a further problem about
words that we have not yet considered. It is that in many languages words have, or may be said to have, many different forms.
In English, for instance, the verb 'to take' is said to have the
forms *take*, *takes*, *took*, *taking* and *taken* (and perhaps *taker*).
Similarly, but perhaps less obviously, the word 'cat' has the two
forms *cat* and *cats*.

We have to be a little careful here about our terminology because the word 'word' is often used in two different senses. We
can talk about the words *cat* and *cats* yet at the same time about
the word 'cat' which has a singular form *cat* and a plural form
cats. In the former, *cat* and *cats* are different words, while in the
latter they are forms of the same word. Obviously we ought to
distinguish between words and forms of words. We might talk
about the word 'cat' and say that it has two forms *cat* and *cats*

so that *cats* is not a word at all, but one form of the word. But this is, of course, to define 'word' in a way quite different from the usage in the previous section. An alternative way of handling the problem is to say that *cat* and *cats* are different words (not just different forms), and to find a new term for 'cat' which covers them both. One suggested term is 'lexeme'. Whichever alternative we choose we shall restrict the use of 'word' to one or other of the possible meanings. The best way to avoid confusion, however, is not to lay down strict rules about the use of terms but to use a different way of indicating 'words' in each of the two senses. I shall do this by using capital letters for CAT and italics for *cat* and *cats*, capitals that is to say for words (= lexemes) and italics for words (= forms of words). (I shall not use the term 'lexeme' and shall use only where there is any danger of confusion, the contrast between 'words' and 'forms of words'.)

There might seem, perhaps, not to be the same confusion with verbs because we talk about 'the verb "to take"' with its various forms but would not describe 'to take' as a word since it is clearly two words. But there is still the problem, because we often speak of the verb 'to take' and also of *takes* as a verb. We want to say that *to take* (as well as *takes* and *take*) is one of the forms of the verb 'to take'. Supposing, for instance, that we say that *kept* cannot be followed by 'to seem', is this meant to imply that we cannot follow *kept* by the form *to seem*, i.e. that there is no *he kept to seem . . . (which is obviously true), or that *kept* cannot be followed by one of the forms of the verb 'to seem', e.g. *seeming*, i.e. that there is no *he kept seeming . . . (which might seem plausible but is almost certainly untrue)? What we need of course is the distinction between TO SEEM the verb and *to seem* the form of the verb.

We really do not then need to refer in English to the verb TO TAKE, but to the verb TAKE. The choice of TO TAKE as the name for the verb, the so called 'infinitive', is probably based on the needs of languages other than English, e.g. French *aimer*, Italian *amare* 'to love'. Not only is TAKE without TO quite sufficient for English, but also we run into difficulties if we try to refer to the auxiliary verbs by a TO ('infinitive') form. A French scholar in fact once referred to the English verbs 'to will' and 'to shall', though of course no such forms exist. And we can have the same kind of fun with the other auxiliaries 'to can', 'to may', 'to must' and 'to ought'. In fact except for the last these forms exist in English, but bear no relation at all to the auxiliaries. What we can, and must do, of course, is to talk of the auxiliaries WILL, SHALL, CAN, MAY, MUST and OUGHT.

The way in which the verb is referred to in grammar books varies according to the language. For Latin the forms meaning 'I advise', 'I love', 'I take', etc. are chosen – the form *amo* is used to refer to the verb AMO. For Semitic languages it would be the form meaning 'he loves', for French or Russian the form meaning 'to love'. The form I have chosen for English, *love* (for the verb LOVE), is the 'simple' or 'unmarked' form which is used in a variety of positions where other languages use the 'infinitive' or the 'imperative' or even one of the forms of the present tense. This can be shown by *come* in:

> *I saw him come.*
> *Come here at once.*
> *I come every day.*

The variations in the form of a word was called 'inflection' in the traditional grammars. In more recent linguistic works it is referred to as *morphology*, 'the study of forms'.

Most of the languages with which we are familiar have a far more complex morphology than English. Latin, for instance, has about 120 forms of the verb, beginning, as generations of schoolboys have learnt, with *amo, amas, amat, amamus, amatis, amant*. But equally French, German, Italian and most other European languages have far more forms than English which (except with BE) never has more than five different forms of the verb, e.g. *take, takes, taking, took, taken*, and often only three, e.g. *hit, hits, hitting*. Many other languages have highly complex verb morphology, e.g. the Bantu languages such as Nyanja, Kikuyu and Swahili, and many of the American Indian languages.

More striking, perhaps, is that many languages have many

forms of the noun though, apart from the possessive forms, English has never more than two, the singular and the plural (unless we count the small number which appear to have two plurals, e.g. *brother*, *brothers*, *brethren*; *index*, *indexes*, *indices*). But Latin nouns have usually seven or eight different forms because of Latin's 'case' system. The way that they are set out in the grammar books (in 'paradigms') suggests that there might be twelve different forms but some of the forms appear more than once, e.g.

	SINGULAR	PLURAL
nominative	*amicus* (friend)	*amici*
vocative	*amice*	*amici*
accusative	*amicum*	*amicos*
genitive	*amici*	*amicorum*
dative	*amico*	*amicis*
ablative	*amico*	*amicis*

The Latin adjectives have considerably more forms since adjectives can be masculine, feminine or neuter. The number of forms listed in the paradigms is thirty-six though the number of actually different forms is only fourteen.

Some languages, such as Chinese, as we saw in the first chapter, have no distinct forms of words at all. They have no inflection, no morphology. There are other languages, however, which, though they have many forms of the same word, have a morphology that is very different from that of Latin, French, or even Arabic. In these languages the forms are always made up of clearly identifiable parts. In Swahili, for example, the translation of 'he saw you' is *alikuona*, which seems to be a single word. But it is in fact composed of four parts *a* 'he', *li* past tense, *ku* 'you' and *ona* 'see'. These can be replaced by similar elements, e.g. *ni* for 'I' or 'me', or *ta* for future, so that we can form the words *atakuona* 'he will see you', *nilikuona* 'I saw you', *ataniona* 'he will see me' and so on. All we have to do is to put the correct elements together in the right order. This is very different from Latin where *amo* means 'I love', *amat* 'he loves', *amabam* 'I loved'. There are here no distinct elements for 'I', 'he', present tense or past tense. The term 'inflectional' is used to refer to languages like Latin in which the grammatical elements cannot be separated, while the term for languages like Swahili is 'agglutinative'. There is very little point in writing out paradigms for the Swahili verbs; all we need to do is to list the various elements that make up the word.

The nineteenth-century scholar Wilhelm von Humboldt divided all the languages of the world into three types – 'inflectional', 'agglutinative' and 'isolating'. As we have seen, Latin and Swahili are examples of inflectional and agglutinative languages respectively. An example of an isolating language is Chinese – or any other language that has no morphology. This is not a very useful classification of languages as a whole, for two reasons. First, it refers only to one aspect of the language, the word formation. Secondly, most languages have characteristics of all three types. Swahili, for instance, is not wholly agglutinative, but has some inflection in the strict sense; a better example of an agglutinative language might be Turkish. Classical Greek was highly inflectional. The *-o* of *luo* 'I loose' identifies no less than five categories – person (first person), number (singular), tense (present), mood (indicative) and voice (active). Nevertheless the form *lusontai*, 'they will loose themselves' can be split into six parts (and so treated as a word in an agglutinative language) – *lu* 'loose', *s* future tense, *o* indicative mood, *n* plural number, *t* third person and *ai* middle or passive voice. In English there are words exhibiting all three types. The prepositions, e.g. *by*, *near*, *to*, are 'invariable' and so might have belonged to an isolating language, *see/saw* is an example of inflection, while the forms *love/loves/loved/loving* could all be handled in terms of agglutination. This division into inflectional, agglutinative and isolating cannot then be a division of language types, but only of the morphological characteristics of parts of languages.

It is quite clear from what has been said above and from remarks in the first chapter that morphology does not make up the whole of grammar. We have also to consider what is both traditionally, and in modern linguistics, called 'syntax'. There are, however, two quite distinct areas of syntax, one related to morphology, the other wholly or largely unrelated to it.

First there is an area of syntax that is concerned with the 'selectional restrictions' of concord and government. This we shall deal with in detail in 2.6. It is enough to note here that this deals with the occurrence in very specific linguistic contexts of one form of a word rather than another, of, for instance, *takes* instead of *take* in *He . . . a bath every day*, or of *mensam* or *mensas* rather than any other form of the noun MENSA 'a table' in *. . . videt* 'he sees a table'. (The fact that these different forms exist, as opposed to the fact of their occurrence in specific contexts, is, of course, a matter of morphology.) Secondly syntax is concerned with the order of words. The fact that *John sees Bill* is different from *Bill sees John* shows clearly that the order of words is important in English, and this too is a matter of syntax. More subtly, such ordering may show that words belong to different classes and the class to which a word belongs is a matter of importance. The American linguist Charles Hockett has pointed out that in Chinese *crau³ fan⁴* (the raised figures mark tones, for Chinese is a 'tone' language) may mean either 'to fry rice' or 'fried rice'. But these are different syntactically in that in one *crau³* is a verb and in the other an adjective; the distinction of verb and adjective can be established by the unambiguous *cr¹ fan⁴* 'to eat rice' and *hau³ fan⁴* 'good rice'. A similar example in English is the headline *British bitter wins in Europe*. Is this about the success of bitter ale or about some unhappy victories in football? It depends on whether *bitter wins* is a noun and a verb or adjective and a noun, whether it is to be compared with *bitter fails* or with *happy wins*. Since these are all matters of syntax it follows that it is unlikely that there are any languages without syntax; and there are, therefore, no languages without grammar.

A further point about syntax and morphology is that there are many morphological features that are often not regarded as strictly grammatical, precisely because they do not link up with syntax in the first sense I have mentioned above (i.e. occurrence in very specific contexts). In this sense the occurrence of *believe* and *believes* is dependent on the occurrence of *men* vs. *man* in *the men believe* but *the man believes*. This is the relationship known as 'agreement' or 'concord'. Nouns are said to 'agree with' verbs in number – both must be singular or plural, though it may be noted that this is true in English of the present tense only, for in the past we have both *the men believed* and *the man believed*. But what of the distinction between *belief* and *believe*? This is usually treated as something different, as 'derivation', while the term 'inflection' is reserved for those morphological features that more obviously involve syntax. Derivation often entails a change from one word class ('part of speech') to another, as in the example I have quoted, since *belief* is a noun and *believe* is a verb, and it is often very irregular with many quite different types of formation – *think/thought*, *attend/attention*, *please/pleasure*, etc. These are usually regarded as different words, not merely as different forms of the same word. They do not always involve a change of word class; both *professor* and *professorship* are nouns. The distinction between inflection and derivation is not always clear. Is *nice/nicer/nicest* inflection or derivation? It does not involve us in syntax, but it seems to be more a matter of forms of the same word than of different words related by derivation. It is not important that we cannot easily decide; we cannot always draw clear distinctions in linguistics – it is more often a matter of convenience than of any kind of truth.

The traditional grammars deal with morphology in what is sometimes called the 'word and paradigm' approach. A single word such as Latin AMO has all its forms set out in lists – paradigms:

amo	I love
amas	thou lovest
amat	he loves
amamus	we love
amatis	you love
amant	they love

and so on, throughout all the tenses, moods and voices of Latin, a sum total of at least 120 forms.

This is not a wholly satisfactory approach for several reasons. First it relies too much on the intuition of the student. For he is merely told that AMO is a 'first conjugation verb', that MONEO

'I advise' is a 'second conjugation verb' and so on, and then is expected to work out for himself the forms of LAUDO 'I praise' on the analogy of AMO. In other words he is never told precisely what are the forms of the other verbs of Latin; he is left to deduce for himself the points of similarity and difference. What is important, one would have thought, is not the forms of AMO, but the endings of all the verbs of this 'first conjugation'. Moreover, when the schoolboy learns REGO 'I rule' (third conjugation) and AUDIO 'I hear' (fourth conjugation) he is given a decreasing amount of time to learn them because they differ from AMO in certain fairly clearly establishable ways – partly that where AMO has an -a- and MONEO an -e-, REGO has various short vowels and AUDIO an -i-. The student is not told this; he is left to work it out for himself. This may be good exercise for the brain, but it is not good linguistics. What we need then is a precise and explicit statement of the way in which the forms are related to one another, and this we do not find in a 'word and paradigm' grammar. We shall consider some alternatives later.

2.3 Parts of speech

The traditional grammars often began with a statement of the 'parts of speech', which today would be called 'word classes'. According to most grammars there are eight parts of speech. They are (with typical examples):

noun	(*howling, wolf, flock, terror*)
pronoun	(*I, you, he, which*)
adjective	(*this, the, fourth, each, untidy*)
verb	(*see, retire, laugh*)
preposition	(*on, in, to*)
conjunction	(*and, but, because*)
adverb	(*much, deservedly, partly, merely*)
interjection	(*alas*)

This kind of classification goes back to the Greek philosophers Plato and Aristotle, though the first really clear statement comes from the most famous of Greek grammarians, Dionysius Thrax, who produced a grammar of Greek in about 100 B.C. Dionysius also recognized eight parts of speech. Six of them were identical with those listed above; the only difference in the more modern list is that it has distinguished nouns and adjectives and added the interjections, omitting the participle and the article as separate parts of speech. It is never very clear in the grammars why these eight parts of speech must be stressed; they do not appear to be an essential prerequisite for the rest of the grammar, but are introduced rather as an academic exercise. Like so much of what is to be found in these grammars they are there because of the classical tradition and because their justification was never seriously challenged. There are, however, quite serious objections to this traditional classification.

First, the definitions are largely notional and often extremely vague. It would in fact often be quite impossible to judge from these definitions whether a particular word was a noun, a verb or an adjective without knowing the answer already! We have discussed Nesfield's definition of a noun on pp. 39–40 and seen how totally circular it was. His definition of the verb is even worse because it is utterly uninformative – 'A verb is a word used for *saying* something about something else.' Do not most words say something about something else? His definitions of the pronoun and the adjective are a little better: 'A pronoun is a word used instead of a noun', 'An adjective is a word used to qualify a noun.' They are almost definitions in purely grammatical terms, as they should be, but they are still not precise enough. If we consider the pronoun we can see that many kinds of word may be used instead of the noun *John*:

John came this morning.
A man/Someone/You-know-who/The aforementioned came this morning.

In the definition of the adjective what does 'qualify' mean? Precede? Either precede or follow? Is *John's* an adjective in *John's book*? Is *there* an adjective in *the people there*? (See more on this on p. 65.) It is interesting to note that the definitions given by Dionysius Thrax almost two thousand years ago were formal, based largely upon morphology (though we may well question whether morphology ought to determine word classes – see p. 69). It was for this reason that he placed noun and adjective in the same class, because in Greek both have case endings.

Secondly, the number of parts of speech in the traditional grammars seems to be quite arbitrary. Why eight? Probably because Dionysius Thrax had eight. The adverb in particular is a most peculiar class. It is quite clearly a 'rag bag' or 'dustbin', the class into which words that do not seem to belong elsewhere are placed. This is easily illustrated by considering *very* and *quickly*, both of which are traditionally considered to be adverbs. They have almost nothing in common as shown by the following pairs of possible and impossible sentences (the latter marked with asterisks):

> *He ran away quickly.*
> **He ran away very.*
> *He is very good.*
> **He is quickly good.*
> *He has a very fast car.*
> **He has a quickly fast car.*

We can overcome this problem if we wish by recognizing two different classes, one of 'adverbs' – *quickly, beautifully* etc. the other of 'intensifiers': *very, fairly, quite*, etc. But we are then faced with the problem of the status of other rather similar words like *usually*. Is this an adverb in the same (though restricted sense) in which *quickly* is? Again let us look at some sentences:

> **He ran away usually* (but *He usually ran away*).
> *He ran away quickly.*
> *He is usually good.*
> **He is quickly good.*
> **He has a usually fast car.*
> **He has a quickly fast car.*

It would appear, then, that we need far more classes than eight. The American scholar C. C. Fries suggested in his book *The Structure of English* that English had four parts of speech and fifteen groups of 'form words'. The four parts of speech he labelled classes 1, 2, 3 and 4, but they are clearly what would normally be called 'nouns', 'verbs', 'adjectives' and 'adverbs'. Fries was at pains to warn the reader against this identification of his classes with these traditional parts of speech, because he wanted to insist that his theoretical framework was different from that of the traditional grammars. We need not be too concerned about this; there is much to be said for retaining the old terms simply because it is so much easier to remember them, provided we are careful not to forget that we are using them differently. A particularly striking point about Fries's classification is that what traditional grammars call adverbs are treated in no less than five of his fifteen groups as well as providing the total membership of his class 4. The correspondences between the two systems of classification are:

FRIES	NESFIELD	EXAMPLE
Class 4	Time	*now*
	Place	*here*
	Number	*once*
	Description	*slowly*
Group C	Affirming or denying	*not*
Group D	Quality, extent or degree	*very*
Group H	Place (introductory)	*there (is/are . . .)*
Group I	Interrogative	*when*
Group L	Affirming or denying	*no*

Nesfield, moreover, divides his interrogative adverbs into those of time, place, number, description, quality or degree, and cause or reason. This should make us wonder first why the interrogative adverbs are 'form words' (Group I) while the corresponding non-interrogative ones are 'parts of speech' for Fries (compare, for instance, *where* and *here*), and secondly why Fries does not sub-classify his Class 4. These 'adverbs' do not all have identical functions, apart from the obvious differences in their meaning. There are difficulties with Fries's classification, but at least he showed that the eight traditional parts of speech are not satisfactory.

G.—4

It is, however, quite impossible to write a grammar of a language without setting up word classes. For not only will the grammar be stated largely in terms of the function of classes of words, but it is essential to indicate in the dictionary precisely how a word functions in the language, and this is done by indicating its class, e.g. that *elephant* is a noun and *depend* a verb. We do not need, however, to define each word class before we start. Rather, the definition of the word class is established by what is said about it in the grammar. In other words if you want to know what a noun is you will have to see what the grammar has to say about the functions of the noun (and if you want to know which words can be called nouns you must, of course, look to the dictionary). The functions may well be many and varied. The noun *boy*, for instance, has a different function in each of the following sentences, and the grammar must specify quite clearly what these functions are:

> *The boy has come.*
> *I've seen the boy.*
> *I gave it to the boy.*
> *This is the boy's mother.*

But by making quite clear that words such as *boy* have these (and other) functions, the grammar provides a definition of the noun. We do not, therefore, need the notional definitions even if we could use them. Similarly we do not give much weight to morphology. What is important about nouns is not that they have singular and plural forms (*boy*, *boys*), but that they have syntactic functions such as those illustrated above. It is quite proper, therefore, that in the brief discussion of word classes that follows we shall have to refer constantly to points of grammar made elsewhere in this book.

The traditional classes constitute, like so many traditional grammatical points, a fairly reasonable interpretation of the English language. The two most important classes are noun and verb. Every complete sentence (see p. 72) must contain at least one word from each class. Thus a sentence such as *Birds fly* is the smallest possible. Apart from the *-er* and *-est* forms of adjectives, words of these two classes alone have morphological features, the noun with two forms and the verb with up to five (*take, takes, took, taken, taking*). The most important sub-classification of the noun is into countables and uncountables (see p. 191), though the pronoun which has special features of its own (see p. 89) is also, perhaps, to be regarded as a sub-class of the noun, since its functions are largely the same. The most important sub-classification of the verb is into auxiliaries and full verbs (see p. 193).

Another major class is the adjective with two main functions, attributive and predicative, as illustrated by *the little boy* and *The boy is little* respectively. But the traditional term 'adjective' includes words that are best regarded as members of a different class. The articles (*the, a*), possessive pronouns (*his, her, my, their,* etc.), demonstratives (*this, that, these, those*), plus words such as *all, some, neither,* which precede the adjectives and most of which are never used predicatively, are treated today as 'determinatives' or 'determiners'.

The adverb we have already discussed. The preposition functions with a noun or rather a noun phrase (see p. 76) as in *to John, on the table,* with the resulting sequence of words functioning like an adverb of time or place. Finally, conjunctions are words that link sentences, though we should, perhaps, distinguish those that coordinate and those that subordinate (see p. 79).

This does not account for all words of English. There are others such as *not, who, yes,* that have very special functions and belong either to a class of their own or to a class with very few members. It is hardly worth while treating these as word classes. The grammar will specify how they function and the dictionary can do no more than refer to the grammar for this specific item. Some scholars have, in fact, made a distinction between 'full' words and 'empty' words (or between 'lexical' and 'grammatical' words) to distinguish such words as these – and others such as the pronouns and, perhaps, the conjunctions or even the prepositions – from those classes such as noun and verb which contain a vast number of 'lexical' items. But there is no precise line of division between them.

Even on this approach, however, several problems arise. The

first results from the fact that some word classes have a variety of functions, but, unfortunately, not all words of the class seem to have all the functions. This problem is well illustrated by the adjective. It will be remembered that we spoke of its attributive and predicative functions as in *the little boy* and *The boy is little*. But there are words that may be used predicatively but not attributively. Examples are *well*, *glad* and possibly *ill* as well as many words that begin with *a-*: *afraid*, *asleep*, *alike*, *awake*, *abroad*. We can say:

> *The boy was well/glad/abroad/afraid*, etc.

but not

> **the well/glad/abroad/afraid*, etc. *boy* ...

The status of *ill* is not wholly clear. Can we or can we not say *the ill boy*? *Glad*, moreover, has an attributive function but only in the 'fixed phrase' which is surely a linguistic 'fossil' – *glad tidings*. On the other side there are some words which may appear in the attributive position but not in the predicative position. Examples are *main*, *mere*, *utter*:

> *the main decision*   but not   **The decision was main,*
> *mere ignorance*   but not   **The ignorance was mere,*
> *utter darkness*   but not   **The darkness was utter.*

Note also that we can say:

> *the top shelf*   but not   **The shelf was top,*

but both:

> *the top boy*   and   *The boy was top.*

There are some words which appear in both positions but do so with quite a different meaning. There is the old joke of the lady who wanted a painting of her late husband and the artist who replied that he did not mind waiting for him. We may also note, for a difference in meaning:

> *the right girl/The girl was right.*
> *my old friend/My friend was old.*

As we have seen, there is a similar problem with *a heavy smoker* which is not related to *The smoker was heavy* and similarly with *a hard worker*, *a poor loser*, *a bad singer*, etc. For many of these, in fact, it is quite clear that the related sentence is not of the type *The smoker was heavy* but *He smokes heavily*, i.e. that the attributive adjective is not in any way to be associated with a predicative adjective but with an adverb.

We shall have similar difficulties if we treat the so-called ordinal numerals – *first*, *second*, *last*, etc. – as adjectives. For we cannot relate:

> *The Frenchman was first/second/last* with
> *the first/second/last Frenchman.*

But, perhaps, we might not treat these as adjectives at all but as determinatives along with *the*, *this*, *some*, etc.

We might, because of this, be tempted to say that only predicative functions should be used as a true test of the adjective, or at least to regard this as the basic function. In fact, in the early form of transformational grammar (see p. 135) it was thought that *the good boy* should be derived from *The boy is good*. This should have the advantage that we could deal with *the heavy smoker* in a different way by deriving it from *He smokes heavily*, the attributive function thus being derived in different ways in English. But again there are difficulties. We can easily go too far. We might be tempted to say that in that case *abroad* and *asleep* were true adjectives, though of a special kind which in attributive position followed their noun instead of preceding it as in *people abroad*, *children asleep*. In view of the fact that most adjectives in French follow the noun this would seem quite plausible. It then might follow that *here* and *there* are also adjectives in view of:

> *The men are here/there.*
> *the men here/there.*

Equally we shall have to treat *in the garden* as an adjectival phrase in view of:

> *The children are in the garden.*
> *the children in the garden.*

Clearly we should be doubtful about this statement. In some recent linguistics works words such as *abroad* are treated as 'adjuncts' rather than as adjectives; semantically most of them are distinguished as place and time markers. But there are some words of this kind that may occupy the position before the noun as well as after it – *upstairs, inside,* etc.:

> *the upstairs room/the room upstairs*
> *the inside wall/the wall inside*

Are these adjectives in the first example but adjuncts in the second?

There are other features that may be associated with adjectives and perhaps used as criteria for establishing this class. First, they may be preceded by words like *very*. This could be said to be quite an important criterion; we can clearly establish that *interesting* is an adjective while *singing* is not by using the *very* test:

> *The book is interesting/very interesting.*
> *The bird is singing/*very singing.*
> *The interesting/very interesting book.*
> *The singing/*very singing bird.*

The occurrence of *very* in *very interesting* is important because without it we might be tempted to say that in *This book is interesting, is interesting* is all part of the verb as in *The bird is singing,* though we would normally expect a verb such as *interesting* to have an object as in *This book is interesting me.* We find that many verbs of a similar type, *frighten, shock, please,* etc. function in just the same way – *This book is frightening/shocking* and also *very frightening/shocking.* We must say, then, that with these the *-ing* form is a true adjective – formed by derivation. But to return to our previous examples, we find we can say *The boy is very glad/well/afraid* but not ... *very abroad* nor, except perhaps in joking form, ... *very asleep* or *very awake.* This test does not, then, give us any clear answers. It would permit us to treat *afraid* as an adjective but to exclude *abroad,* although on the previous predicative/attributive tests these would seem to pass or fail together. It would also exclude *upstairs, inside,* etc., which have the maximum freedom of occurrence – before the noun, after the noun, and in the predicative position, yet would include *top* and *bottom* which are far more restricted:

> *the top shelf/the very top shelf,*

but not

> **The shelf was top.*

Clearly, then, occurrence with *very* will not give us a clear decision whether a word is or is not an adjective.

A further possible criterion for the adjective is that it has 'comparative' and 'superlative' forms – *nice, nicer, nicest* and *beautiful, more beautiful, most beautiful*. It should be remembered first, however, that some of the words described as adverbs have similar forms *fast, faster, fastest*, and *quickly, more quickly, most quickly*. This test will exclude most of the 'doubtful' words – *here, there, abroad, asleep*, etc., *downstairs, inside*, etc., *top* and *bottom*, as well as *main, mere, utter* and in the attributive function *right, late* (but not *old – an older friend*). And it will permit us to treat *heavy* and *bad* as adjectives in *heavy smoker* and *bad singer*. But is this perhaps not too restrictive a criterion? We shall be left with only the really 'central' class of adjectives.

The difficulties we have been discussing arise from the fact that not all words that we want to put in a single class seem to have all the functions of that class. There is another problem that arises from what is almost the converse situation, that some words seem to belong to more than one class. Examples of this are *steel* and *cotton* in *Steel is strong*, *a steel bridge* and *Cotton comes from Egypt* and *a cotton shirt*. In the first of each pair the words would seem to be nouns, in the second they seem to be adjectives. Some decades ago there was a famous argument over the question whether these were adjectives or nouns being used as adjectives. One answer that is sometimes given is that we must distinguish between the word class and the function – that we here have the word class noun, and the function 'modifier' which is not to be identified with adjective. All we have to say then is that nouns may be used as modifiers as well as in their more usual function as 'heads' of noun phrases. *Steel* would be a modifier in *steel bridge* though a head in *fine steel*, with *fine* as a modifier. But this is largely a terminological way out; we could have decided to say that *steel* is an adjective as well as a noun. There is a further possibility, that it is an adjective being used as a noun. This may seem less plausible for *steel* but more plausible for *poor* in *The poor are always with us* or for *blues* in *the blues*. Are not *poor* and *blue* adjectives being used as nouns? There is no definite answer to this problem but the most plausible solution is that *steel*, *cotton*, etc. are nouns, but 'nouns of material', and that such nouns may be used in an adjectival function to mean 'made of . . .' and that similarly adjectives like *poor*, *wicked*, *good*, etc. (in fact all adjectives that can be followed by *people*), may be used with the function of nouns in *the poor*, etc. The colour adjectives may be used in a similar way with the additional feature that they then have both singular and plural forms, since we have *the blue* and *the blues*, but only *the poor* and not **the poors*. We have to make a decision, then, to place these words in the class of noun or adjective but to sub-classify to show that they sometimes have functions of the other class. The decision to treat them all as 'basically' nouns or adjectives is one that can certainly be justified in a practical way. It is simpler to list *steel*, *cotton*, etc., as a sub-class of nouns with adjective-like function rather than list them twice, first as nouns and then as adjectives.

While we are considering this function of nouns acting as adjectives we ought to consider the status of the first words in *bus stop*, *shoe polish*, *bread shop*, etc. The point here is that in English any noun can be placed before another noun with a kind of prepositional meaning – 'a stop for buses', 'polish for shoes'. We can extend the list of nouns so placed together almost ad infinitum *bus stop girl*, *bus stop girl inquiry*, *bus stop girl inquiry row*, etc., though these are more typical of newspaper headlines than of ordinary English. But here we do not need to talk about adjectival function, because this is a function of all nouns. Complexes of this kind are a feature of grammar. The noun-noun sequence is, perhaps, a particularly English feature, but raises no new problems of description. Note, in particular, the adjectival function of *steel* in *steel bridge* and the purely nominal complex of *steel company*. The stress marks this distinction quite clearly since in the latter the main stress falls on *steel* (compare also *silver* in *silver box* to mean either '*box* made of *silver*' or '*box* for *silver*').

There are other words that we would wish to consider as belonging to several different classes. *Love* and *work* in English seem to be both noun and verb, *safe* and *choice* to be both adjective and noun. *Round* seems to be a noun, an adjective, a verb, a preposition and an adverb – *a round of toast, a round ball, to round the Horn, round the mulberry bush* and *make it go round*! We could of course, if we wished, say that these belong to the rather special classes of noun-verb, adjective-noun, noun-adjective-verb-preposition-adverb. This would certainly save us listing them more than once in each class. This solution was quite seriously suggested by Hockett who recognized seven major classes – N, A, V, NA, NV, AV and NAV – plus an eighth, particles. But in practice this is a pointless difference. We shall never need to list all the members of each class. Rather we shall list (in the dictionary) all the words of the language and nothing at all is gained by stating that *work* belongs to the class NV rather than that it belongs to the classes N and V.

A final problem involves us in, again, consideration of morphology. It has been assumed throughout this section that word classes are classes of words in the sense in which CAT is a word, not *cat* and *cats*. It is for this reason that some scholars (beginning with Dionysius Thrax) have used morphological criteria for setting up word classes. Hockett, for instance, divided the words of Nootka (North American Indian) into *inflected* and *uninflected*, a purely morphological division. But it is obvious that the main purpose of setting up word classes is to state how they function in the language, to class the words in terms of their syntactic function, and this we have been trying to do in this section. The status of *steel, cotton, blue, poor* was very largely discussed in terms of the places in which they occur (though we also noted the morphological point of *blue/blues*). But a problem arises from the fact that some of the forms of the same word have quite different syntactic functions, functions that relate to different word classes. 'Participles' and 'verbal nouns', for instance, such as *singing*, *playing* in English, or *amans*, *amaturus*, *amandum*, *amatus*, *amare* in Latin, seem to be forms of verbs, but to have the function of nouns or adjectives. Do we then say they are not inflected forms, but derived forms like *singer*? Are they nouns or adjectives derived from verbs, since derivation often involves change of word class? The answer must surely be 'no'. Just as we can class *steel* as a noun and permit it to have adjective-like function, so we must write the grammar in such a way that certain forms of verbs (not all the forms of the whole verb – and this is why we have a different situation from that of *steel*) may function as nouns or adjectives. There is a rather striking situation in the Cushitic (Ethiopian) language Bilin. The genitive ('possessive') forms of the noun function like adjectives and have all the morphological features of the adjective. For instance, the word for *man* is *gerwa* and the word for *man's* is *gerwix*^{w} but *gerwix*^{w} is not only the genitive of *gerwa* but is also an adjective in the nominative case. If we want to say *to the man's mother*, not only does the word for *mother* have to be placed in the dative case, but also the word for *the man's*, since it is an adjective; the form is *gerwix*^{w}*əd*. In this language forms of nouns not only function like adjectives syntactically, but also regularly have the morphology of the adjective, as well as retaining the morphology of the noun! And the same is true of verb forms which have adjectival function. The Bilin system is very neat and there is no difficulty, provided we do not ask whether its forms are 'really' verbs and nouns or 'really' adjectives. They belong to the class of verb or noun because that is how we must mark them in the dictionary, but our grammar will show that both syntactically and morphologically they have the function of adjectives.

2.4 Sentence, clause and phrase

In traditional grammars 'sentence' like 'word' is a basic though largely undefined term. Sentences are thus simply 'composed of words', and it is the function of syntax to state what words can be combined with others to form sentences and in what order.

Most people are quite clear in their own mind that they know exactly what a sentence is. This confidence arises because in a literate society we are taught to indicate sentences in our writing by putting in the punctuation. The normal mark of the sentence is the full stop; it would be an error of punctuation to mark the end of a sentence with a comma. In addition new sentences must begin with capital letters. This does not, however, help us to understand what a sentence is. It certainly does not give us a definition. In fact, we are taught at school to recognize sentences through practice, not by a set of rules.

The traditional grammars, however, sometimes provide a kind of definition: a sentence is the expression of a complete thought. But this is notional and shares all the faults of the notional definitions that we discussed in Chapter 1. How do we know what a complete thought is? Is 'cabbage' or 'man' a complete thought? If not, why not? And is *If it rains I shan't come* one thought, or two joined together? It would seem quite impossible to provide any definition along these lines. Equally it is impossible to provide a logical definition for the sentence. One such would be that it contains a subject and predicate – that on the one hand it indicates something that we are talking about, and on the other it says something about it. For instance, in *John is coming* we are talking about John, the subject, and also saying that he is coming, the predicate. The difficulty here is that if this definition is to be of any use we must be able to identify what we are talking about, and very often we talk about several things at once. For instance, in the sentence *John gave the book to Mary* we are clearly talking about *John*, *the book* and *Mary* and all three might seem to be the 'subject' in this sense. A natural reaction, especially from someone who has learnt some traditional grammar, might be to say that we are talking about John and that what we are saying about him is that he gave the book to Mary. But this begs the question. It defines the subject as the GRAMMATICAL subject, and the grammatical subject can only be defined in terms of the sentence. Moreover the grammatical subject often does not indicate what we are 'talking about'. In *The birds have eaten all the fruit* it is probable that what we are talking about is the missing fruit and not the unidentified birds! More strikingly, in *It's rain-ing* what is the subject? *It*? But what is 'It'? – the weather, the universe, or what? Clearly no definition of sentence in terms of such logical concepts is going to help, though (and this is an im-portant caveat) once we have established what a sentence is we may well look to see if it can be interpreted in terms of a subject and a predicate (defined GRAMMATICALLY).

Even if we have learnt by some means or other at school to put our full stops and our capital letters in the right places and even if, therefore, it is possible to establish just how many sentences there are on the page, it would be a mistake to think that speech is equally made up of sentences. As we saw in Chapter 1, although sections of speech are often marked by intonation, it is not the case that every intonation tune will mark a stretch of speech that, if written, would begin with a capital letter and end with a full stop. Moreover a great deal of spoken language does not con-sist of sentences in the sense in which the term is understood for writing at all. Much of it is made up of incomplete, interrupted, unfinished, or even quite chaotic sentences. Speech may be made up of utterances – separate 'bits' – but utterances seldom cor-respond to sentences.

We could not, for instance, identify all the sentences in a con-versation that went:

MARY: John! Coming?

JOHN: Yes dear, I was only –

MARY: Oh do hurry up and – we ought to catch the bus – only they don't always run on time – if we're lucky – wretched people – as long as you're quick. I've been ready for some – since half past seven.

Such a conversation is not abnormal; much of our everyday speech is like this.

A linguistic definition of the sentence must, in fact, be in terms of its internal structure. A sentence will be composed of certain specified elements in a certain order, ultimately, of course, of words or parts of words. A statement then of the structures will provide us with a definition of the sentence. For instance, we might argue that the basic sentence structures of English are of the type NV, NVA, NVN, NVNN, where A stands for adjective. Examples would be *John came*, *John is good*, *John saw Bill*, *John made Bill president*. (This is by no means a satisfactorily complete list.) All other sentences could be regarded as derived from these by either addition, e.g. of adverbs – *John came quickly* – or by expansion: instead of *John* we could have *the boy*, *the little boy*, *the silly little boy* and even *the silly little boy on the other side of the room*. Clearly we can state what is possible, and the sentence is then defined in terms of all these possibilities. But even this is not really satisfactory. We can, indeed, say that a sentence is a linguistic item that accords with our description – that has the structure we assign to the sentence. But why these structures? In particular why not much larger structures, e.g. one that would allow a combination of several of those we have been considering? Why do we not want to consider *It's raining, I'm not going out* as a single sentence? The answer is that these sentence structures are the largest that can be handled in a grammatical description. We can make an accurate statement about the structure of a sentence, that is to say about the limitations on the co-occurrence of the items in the sentence, but we cannot with any accuracy deal with larger structures, structures consisting of two or more sentences. This was put quite clearly by Bloomfield, who defined a sentence as 'an independent linguistic form, not included by virtue of any grammatical construction in any larger linguistic form'. He considered the example: *How are you? It's a fine day. Are you going to play tennis this afternoon?* and goes on to show that there are no grammatical restraints linking these into a single structure; they have to be regarded as three separate units, that is to say, three sentences.

In a sense, then, what is meant by sentence is defined in practical terms. It is the largest unit to which we can assign a grammatical structure. Nevertheless it would be an error to believe that outside the sentence there are no restraints, no features that link one sentence to another. There are, on the contrary, plenty. Many words such as *however*, *therefore*, *later*, *other* serve very often to refer from one sentence to another. More striking perhaps are what are sometimes called the 'pro-forms' of a language. Pronouns are familiar enough. *He*, *she* and *it* may 'stand for' *the man*, *the woman*, *the table*, etc. We find in one sentence *The man . . .* but in the next, *He . . .* But there are also 'pro-verbs'. *Did* in *John came and so did Mary* clearly stands for *came* – Mary came. All the auxiliary verbs in English can act as pro-verbs in the sense that they alone stand for the whole of the verbal element of which they are or were only the first word:

John is coming.	*Is he?*
I haven't seen him.	*But I have.*
Must you come?	*I really must.*
He'll have been there.	*No he won't.*

The verb DO is particularly important and special because it is the pro-form used where there is no auxiliary verb:

He came yesterday.	*No, he didn't.*

We must not overstate the restrictions within a sentence. There are not very many restrictions on pronouns. We can say *She lost her hat*, but it is not the case that we cannot say *She lost his hat*, though we can say only *She washed herself* and not *She washed himself*. But in general the limits of the sentence are clear because beyond the sentence the limitations are fewer and less strict. In particular there seems to be no restriction at all on the co-occurrence of one sentence type with another, whereas within sentences there are restrictions on the parts. *Mary loves John* is possible but *Loves Mary John* and *Mary John loves* are not (except in a special kind of poetry). Furthermore, beyond the sentence there is no clear limit at all. In writing we use paragraphs, but what are the rules for paragraphing? There are, perhaps, some vague rules – that we start a new paragraph where we start on a new subject – but one may well suspect that paragraphs are also dictated by purely aesthetic considerations; pages without paragraphs look uninteresting. We may not, perhaps, like Alice, demand conversation or pictures in our books but we DO like paragraphs.

A problem is raised by the incomplete, interrupted 'sentences' that we discussed earlier (p. 72). What are we to do with these? Some linguists have argued that they should be analysed independently and treated as possible structures of the English language. But this would seem to be a mistake, above all because there would then be an infinite number of structures and no grammar could claim even partial completeness. There are, however, three kinds of 'incomplete sentence'.

First, there are those that are caused by interruptions or changes of mind on the part of the speaker. In the imaginary conversation on page 72 we find examples in *I was only* – and *I've been ready for some* –. These raise no problems for grammar; they are genuinely incomplete sentences, understandable and analysable as such. (The linguist may not be altogether uninterested in them, however; he may well want to know whether there are conditions for interrupting, for hesitation, change of mind, etc.)

Secondly, there are incomplete sentences that are dependent on what has gone before. *John*, for instance, might be a reply for *Who did it?* or *Who did you see?* It can therefore be reasonably understood as an incomplete form of *John did it* or *I saw John*. There are two important grammatical points about incomplete sentences of this kind. First, as we have already seen from the examples on page 74 they make extensive use of pro-forms; they are, then, to be analysed in terms of the complete, expanded, 'original' form. Secondly, their characteristics are often found within sentences too, as was illustrated also on page 74. Clearly the formation of these sentences is important, and they must be treated as very closely related to what has preceded: they are 'contextually' conditioned and can only be understood as such.

Thirdly, there are incomplete sentences such as *Coming? Coming! Found them? Got you!* which might seem equally to be shortened forms of *Are you coming? I'm coming! Have you found them? I've got you!* But these are not contextually conditioned; they do not in any way depend on what has gone before. There is therefore a case for treating them as English sentences in their own right. Indeed, some linguists would argue that there is no more reason to derive *Coming?* from *Are you coming?* than to suppose that the latter is an expanded form of the former. Generally in grammar we treat simpler forms as more basic. But there is an argument for treating these as derived from the longer forms by 'deletion' – we 'delete' the pronoun and the auxiliary verb. By a similar argument we delete *you* in all the imperative forms. *Come here!* is derived from *You come here!* This analysis is firmly advocated by many linguists (see Chapter **5**), but it is an open question whether we should or should not derive one sentence of this kind from another.

The sentence consists of words, but the words are grouped into elements that are smaller than the sentence. For these most linguists use the term 'phrase'. Sentences are thus analysable into phrases. The most important phrases of the sentences are the verb phrases and the noun phrases (symbolized as VP and NP respectively), e.g.

> *John likes Mary* (NP VP NP).

A phrase in this sense can be a single word, but the phrases are often much longer than single words:

The little boy has been reading a fairy story (NP VP NP).

In addition there are elements within the sentence such as *this morning* or *in the garden* which are sometimes called 'adjuncts' but are better called 'adverbial' phrases.

The structure of the noun phrase and the verb phrase will vary from language to language. If we consider the 'simple' phrases (for complex phrases, see below, p. 133) of English, we find that a noun phrase consists either of a pronoun alone (or, rarely, with an adjective, e.g. *Poor you!*), or of a noun preceded by various words some of which are adjectives and others determinatives (*the*, *this*, *may*, etc.), and sometimes followed by a word such as *abroad* or *asleep* (*people abroad*, *children asleep*). In fact the modifiers of the noun phrase, all the words that is to say except the noun itself, are of numerous and varied types. In particular they have their own place in the sequence. Not only can we not place *asleep* before the noun *asleep children*, but we have to put the adjectives in the right order – *little red hen*, not *red little hen* – putting also any other elements before or after the adjectives and in their right order. This is clearly shown by the following sequences which permit little or no variation:

> *All the twenty-five little English children.*
> *Both her worn-out red cotton dresses.*

The study of the noun phrase itself is worthy of a complete book.

So too is the verb phrase. Its structure is a little less complex in some ways, somewhat more complex in others. The maximum length of a verb phrase seems to be five words, e.g.:

> *He may have been being beaten,*

though it may be doubted whether all five often occur together. There are certainly five elements that occur in sequence:

(1) a 'modal' – WILL, SHALL, CAN, MAY, MUST, OUGHT TO, followed by the simple form of a verb.

(2) HAVE followed by the past participle (the perfect).

(3) BE followed by the *-ing* form of the verb (the 'progressive' or 'continuous').

(4) BE followed by the past participle (the passive).

(5) the main verb.

We can choose any combination of these, provided that, as with the noun phrase, there is a 'head' – the main verb.

It is at this level (or 'rank' – the technical term sometimes used to distinguish a sentence, phrase, word), the level of phrase, that we can talk about 'subjects' and 'objects'. Traditional grammar talks about nouns or noun phrases being subjects or objects of verbs, e.g. in *John loves Mary, John* is the subject and *Mary* the object of *loves*. In English we can, in fact, define 'subject' and 'object' in terms of the position of the noun phrase in the sentence and also in terms of 'agreement' of the subject with the verb (see p. 98). But notice that we should not now talk about 'verb' in this context. It is an error to analyse *John loves Mary* into subject-verb-object. This confuses two kinds of classification. 'Subject' and 'object' refer to sentence elements while 'verb' is the name of a word class like 'noun'. So we must either say that this sentence consists of noun-verb-noun, or more strictly of NP –

VP – NP or else we must find a new name for the sentence element denoted by the verb. One suggested is 'predicator'. We can, therefore, consider that the sentence elements are subject-predicator-object.

We can and must define subjects and objects in terms of their functions within the sentence. We have already seen (p. 71) that it is impossible to define subject and predicate logically. It would be even more difficult to define object as well in this way. Nor can we define the subject as the 'actor', the person who performs the action, and the object the 'goal' or 'recipient', the person or thing that is affected by it. This would not allow us to identify the subject as *John* in any of the following sentences, for in none of them is *John* 'acting' in any intelligible sense:

> *John suffered terribly.*
> *John looked sad.*
> *John saw his brother.*
> *John sank under the waves.*

It would be equally impossible to determine the subject in

> *John lent a book to Bill.*

in view of

> *Bill borrowed a book from John.*

Who is the actor, who the recipient? If *John* is the subject in the first sentence, *Bill* cannot be the subject in the second as long as we rely on purely notional definitions. But there is no real doubt in linguistic terms – in terms of position in the sentence.

Traditional grammars also talk of 'clauses', which are 'sentences that are part of larger sentences'. This definition is, strictly, self-contradictory, but it still indicates what is meant, and illustrates a very important characteristic of natural languages. In, for instance, *John stood still and Mary ran away* we have a 'larger-sentence' consisting of two sentences joined together by *and*. Similarly in *While John was standing there Mary ran away* there are two sentences, the first introduced by *while*, making up the larger sentence.

However, these two larger sentences are different, and illustrate two quite different ways in which sentences may be joined together. In the first, they are simply linked by *and*, and we can link as many as we wish in this way. Moreover, the relationship between the two sentences is not very different from that of two sentences separated by a full stop. There would be little difference in, for instance, *John stood still. Mary ran away.* (It is not true, however, that we can link any two sentences with *and*. We cannot say **Come here and John has arrived* though we can say *Come here. John has arrived.* But, for the most part, there are few restrictions on sentences joined by *and*.) This kind of linking of sentences is known as 'coordination'.

The second way in which two sentences may form a larger sentence is one in which, instead of the two sentences being joined together as equals, one of the sentences functions as part of the other. For instance, alongside *He said many things*, we can say *He said that he was coming*. Clearly *that he was coming* has the same kind of function as *many things*. It is, in fact, the object of the sentence *He said ...* So here we find one sentence taking the place of part of a sentence. This feature linguists have known by a variety of names – 'rank-shifting', 'downgrading' and more recently 'embedding' – one sentence, that is to say, is embedded in another. The traditional grammars referred to this as 'subordination' and talked about the embedded sentence as a 'subordinate clause'. These subordinate clauses were further classified into noun-clauses, adjective-clauses and adverb-clauses, according to whether they had the function of nouns, adjectives or adverbs within the other sentence (the 'main' clause). For instance, in the example we have just mentioned *that he was coming* has the function of a noun, for it is nouns and noun phrases that act as objects. An example of an adjective clause would be *who was standing there* in *The boy who was standing there ran away*. It has a function similar to that of *little* in *the little boy*, though the rules of English permit *little* to come before *boy* but the adjective clause to come after it. An adverb clause would be *while I was standing there* which has the same kind of function as *yesterday* in *I saw John while I was standing there*.

The traditional grammars, then, reserve the term sentence for the 'larger sentence' and talk about the sentences of which it is composed as 'clauses'. But there is really very little to be gained by introducing this new term 'clause', because it is needed only to deal with the problems of subordination, and this is better seen in terms of embedding one sentence within another. A sentence with another sentence embedded in it is still a sentence. There is not much to be gained by treating it as a sentence consisting of two clauses. In the case of coordinate sentences there is even less reason for distinguishing between sentence and clause since we can coordinate other linguistic elements too, for example noun phrases – *the little boy and the big girl* – and we surely do not want a different name for the whole phrase and the two smaller phrases of which it is made up.

The grammars make a distinction, moreover, between 'clause' and 'phrase', though not using 'phrase' in the sense in which I have used it (to distinguish the essential parts of a sentence – the noun phrase, the verb phrase, etc.), but to refer (amongst other things) to a special kind of embedded sentence – one without a finite verb. A 'finite verb' is a verb form that can stand alone in an independent sentence – *comes* is finite but *coming* is not, since we can say *He comes every day* but not *He coming every day*. We are told therefore that *how to do this* in *I don't know how to do this* is a noun phrase, not a noun clause, because it has no finite verb. But this seems an unimportant distinction. There are all sorts of rules for embedding or subordination, but what is important is that the embedded sentence has still many of the characteristics of a sentence. In the example above we still have a predicator *do* and object *this*. In *I don't like John doing that* we have *John* (subject) *doing* (predicator) and *that* (object) – an almost normal sentence, but without a finite form of a verb. We shall discuss some of these problems again later.

In this chapter we have talked about 'analysing' sentences. Traditional grammar made analysis or 'parsing', as it was often called, an essential exercise. In Nesfield, for instance, we are instructed to divide a sentence first into subject and predicate, then to divide the subject into nominative and its enlargement and finally its predicate into finite verb, completion and extension, the

completion being either object or complement or both. For the
sentences *The new master soon put the class into good order* and *A
bird in the hand is worth two in the bush* the analysis is:

1. Subject		2. Predicate			
Nominative or Equivalent	Enlargement	Finite verb	Completion		Extension
			Object	Complement	
master	(1) The (2) new	put	the class	into good order	soon
bird	(1) A (2) in the hand	is	–	worth two in the bush	–

This certainly does indicate in some degree the 'structure' of
the sentence, though we shall be criticizing attempts to analyse
language structurally in the next chapter. But it is, even within
its own lights, far from satisfactory. Why, for instance, do we
have enlargement only for the nominative? The enlargement includes all of what today would be called the modifier of the noun –
the article and the adjective, etc. But ALL nouns in the sentence
may have similar modifiers too. *The* occurs as a modifier in *the
class* which is the object, and in *the bush* which is part of the
complement, and nouns can equally occur in the extension as
part of prepositional phrases. It is misleading too to talk about
'completions' which are required, according to Nesfield, because
some verbs 'do not make sense in themselves' but need either
objects (the transitive verbs) or complements (the copulative
verbs). For there are verbs which seem also to require extensions.
An example is *to lie* (as in *to lie down*) which needs such extensions
as *there* or *on the table* (*it lay there/on the table*). In fact, if we
investigate carefully we shall find that verbs can be classified into

a number of different types requiring various kinds of following elements. We need to recognize at least six different sentence structures exemplified by:

(1) *John signs* (NV).
(2) *John is happy* (NVAdj).
(3) *John is a man* (NVN).
(4) *John hit the man* (NVN).
(5) *John gave the man a book* (NVNN).
(6) *The book is on the table* (NVPrepN).

(3) differs from (4) in that in (3) the verb is what Nesfield calls a 'copulative verb' and what more recent linguists have referred to as a 'linking verb'. We can distinguish it partly because the verbs in the class are largely the same as those of (2), which are followed by adjectives, but more importantly because they have no passive – for (4) we have *The man was hit by John* but for (3) there is no *A man is been by John*. We can, moreover, add to these at least three more:

(7) *The girl made John happy* (NVNAdj).
(8) *The girl made John chairman* (NVNN).
(9) *John put the book on the table* (NVNPrepN).

These three, however, are basically developments from (2), (3) and (4) (by transformation – see pp. 139–41) and are perhaps to be treated as such and not as three new structures.

2.5 Grammatical categories

We mentioned in Chapter 1 the grammatical categories of number, gender and tense. These and others are an essential part of traditional grammar, especially the grammar of the classical languages, though to a varying degree they are also used in the description of modern languages. Some, e.g. gender, are regarded as categories of the noun – nouns are either masculine or feminine (or neuter); others, e.g. tense, are regarded as categories of the verb – past, present, or future; while others, e.g. number, seem to belong to both – in *The boys are* both *boys* and *are* are plural.

There are two respects in which the traditional grammars can be criticized. First, as we have seen, they often define the categories in 'notional' terms. Plural is defined as 'more than one', gender is identified with sex, or tense with time. In spite of this the grammars often produce the same results as an analysis in formal terms; they do not, for instance, fail to recognize *oats* as plural and *wheat* as singular. Secondly, and this too was briefly mentioned, they often take over the categories of Latin and impose them upon English or whatever language they are describing, though they are quite inappropriate, and they pay little or no attention to important categories of the language if such categories are not found in the classical languages.

In this section I propose to look briefly with examples at some of these grammatical categories. Most of them will be familiar, but others less so, and as we look at less familiar languages we shall find that they have to be interpreted in rather surprising ways. But before proceeding it would be useful to list some of the TRADITIONAL categories with an indication of the term used, the class of word with which it is generally found and the kind of meaning with which it is (sometimes misleadingly) associated.

GENDER masculine, feminine (and commonly neuter) – a feature of nouns, associated with male, female and (for neuter) sexless creatures – but very misleadingly so.

NUMBER singular, plural (and sometimes dual) – a feature of nouns and verbs, associated with 'one' and 'more than one' (dual with 'two').

PERSON first person, second person, third person – a classification of the pronouns and a feature of verbs – *I, we*; *you*; *he, she, it, they*.

TENSE present, past, future – a feature of verbs, associated with time.

MOOD indicative, subjunctive and, in classical Greek, optative – a feature of the verb, associated with statements of fact versus possibility, supposition, etc.

VOICE active and passive – again a feature of the verb largely associated with whether the subject was the 'actor' (the one who performed the action) or the 'goal' (the one at the receiving end).

CASE nominative, vocative, accusative, genitive, dative and ablative – a
feature of the noun, associated with a variety of largely unrelated
semantic and grammatical features, but illustrated by the translations
boy (subject), *O boy*, *boy* (object), *of a boy*, *to* or *for a boy*, *from* or
by a boy.

In Chapter 1 we saw good reason why such categories should
not be defined in notional terms. Gender must not be confused
with sex, number with counting, or tense with time. How then
are such categories defined? The answer lies in treating them as
'morphosyntactic' categories. By this I mean that they are all
marked both morphologically (in the form of the word) and
syntactically, by relations to other words in the sentence – the
selectional restrictions of the kind we shall deal with in 2.6. Let
us look in detail at some of these categories.

Let us first take GENDER. We have already seen examples of
French and German – *le livre* (masculine) 'the book', *la porte*
(feminine) 'the door'; *der Tisch* (masculine) 'the table', *die Tür*
(feminine) 'the door', *das Feuer* (neuter) 'the fire'. In these and
other European languages gender must be defined in terms of the
form of the article and the adjective that accompany the noun.
The article and adjectives are said to 'agree' with the noun.
Similar examples from Spanish are (note that the adjective comes
last):

> *el libro rojo* (masculine)   the red book
> *la puerta roja* (feminine)   the red door

What is important here is that we have the contrast of *el* and *la*
and of the endings *-o* and *-a* and that these are determined by the
noun, *libro* requiring one of each pair, *puerta* the other. Russian
has no articles, but the adjectives agree:

> *novij stul* (masculine)   new chair
> *novaja kniga* (feminine)   new book
> *novoe okno* (neuter)   new window

The point that gender is defined in these languages in terms of
the 'agreement' of the adjective and (in some languages) of the
article cannot be over-emphasized. Yet in some languages it

seems possible to recognize the gender of a word by the shape of the word itself. Thus in both Spanish and Italian words ending in -*o* are usually masculine, and words ending in -*a* are feminine. But there are many exceptions – *el poema*, *il poema* 'the poem', *la mano*, *la mano* 'the hand' (Spanish example first, Italian second). Similarly in Latin the nouns of the first declension all end in -*a* in the nominative and are mostly feminine while the nouns of the second declension all end in -*us* or -*um* and are mainly masculine and neuter respectively. But again we cannot define first declension nouns as feminine and second declension nouns as masculine or neuter according to their endings because *agricola* 'a farmer' (first declenson) is masculine, hence we have *agricola bonus* 'a good farmer' not *agricola bona, while *quercus* 'oak' (second declension) is feminine, and there are many other examples. The neuter nouns, however, all end in -*um* (we are considering only these two declensions) and every noun that ends in -*um* is neuter. But this is exceptional.

In European languages gender does not usually affect the verb – it is only the adjectives and articles that agree with the noun. In Russian, however, there are distinct past tense forms of the verb for masculine and feminine (in the singular):

on pisal	he wrote
ona pisala	she wrote

In many Semitic languages, however, gender (along with person and number) is regularly marked in the verb. In Geez (Classical Ethiopic), for instance, the paradigm of the verb reads:

nagara	he spoke
nagarat	she spoke
nagarka	you (a man) spoke
nagarki	you (a woman) spoke
nagarku	I spoke
nagaru	they (men) spoke
nagara	they (women) spoke
nagarkem	you (men) spoke
nagarken	you (women) spoke
nagarna	we spoke

If we think about the definition of gender in terms of classes of noun with which adjectives and possibly verbs agree, and pay no attention to the non-grammatical feature of sex, gender is found in many other languages in a surprising form. In Swahili, for instance, there are word classes which differ in not only having different prefixes but also in requiring similar differences in the adjectives and the verbs. Thus we find:

mtu mzuri	a fine man
nyumba nzuri	a fine house
kitu kizuri	a fine thing
kasha zuri	a fine chest
mahali pazuri	a fine place
kufa kuzuri	a fine death

In these it will be seen that the word meaning 'fine' (*zuri*) is preceded by *m-*, *n-*, *ki-*, nothing, *pa-* and *ku-* according to the noun with which it agrees. There are, in fact, two other classes which I have not given because in the singular they require the same prefix as the first class (*m-*), but each class of these has a different plural form so that we get also (to take the first class and only one of the other classes):

mtu mzuri	a fine man
watu wazuri	fine men
mti mzuri	a fine tree
miti mizuri	fine trees

But not only do adjectives agree with the nouns; so also do verbs, as in:

mtu mzuri umekuja   the fine man has come

but

kitu kizuri kimefunjika   the fine thing is broken.

Here we see the *m-* class nouns require a verb form with an initial *u-* while the *ki-* class nouns require an initial *ki-*.

There is no reference to sex in Swahili gender. In fact there is not a consistently clear difference of meaning between the various classes, except that the first class refers exclusively to living creatures, to 'animates', while the third class (with *ki-*) refers mostly to small things and the fourth mostly to large things. There are similar classes in some American Indian languages and in these the meanings are rather more surprising. In, for instance, the Algonquian languages there is a distinction between two classes of noun which is shown by the verb – the verb agrees with the noun. These two classes are referred to as 'animate' and 'inanimate' since the former includes all the words for persons and animals and the latter most other words. But an interesting point is that the words for 'raspberry', 'kettle' and 'knee' belong to the animate class. Oddly enough, though 'raspberry' is animate, 'strawberry' is inanimate. This classification is one of gender, if by gender we mean the recognition of classes of noun with agreement of adjectives, verbs, etc. It is precisely because there is no one-to-one correlation between the form and the meaning that we are justified in doing this. We have already seen that in European languages gender does not really equal sex, so why associate it with sex rather than define it in purely grammatical terms? There is equally no difficulty about using the terms 'animate' and 'inanimate' even though the 'animate' includes objects that are not alive. The point is simply that we find these classes and we need to label them. We choose the labels that we are most likely to remember; they are essentially mnemonic and nothing more. (Linguistics is not the only discipline that uses such an approach. The giant panda lives exclusively on bamboo shoots, but is classified zoologically as a carnivore.)

NUMBER, perhaps, raises fewer problems. The European languages seem to have merely the distinction of singular and plural, marked in both the noun and the verb, the verb usually agreeing with the subject. In English this is almost 'extinct' but still to be found in *The boy comes*, *The boys come*. In other European languages there is agreement with article and adjectives as well as the verb – French *le petit garçon*, *les petits garçons*, Italian *il piccolo ragazzo*, *i piccoli ragazzi* 'the little boy', 'the little boys'. Some languages, especially the classical languages, have singular, dual (two) and plural. Classical Greek was

one such, and also Classical Arabic. Thus in Arabic we find
malikun 'a king', *malikāni* 'two kings', *malikūna* 'kings', and if we
look to the verb there are no less than thirteen forms in the
paradigm (for do not forget that gender is marked too):

3 m.s.	*kataba*	he wrote
3 f.s.	*katabat*	she wrote
2 m.s.	*katabta*	you (a man) wrote
2 f.s.	*katabti*	you (woman) wrote
1 m/f.s.	*katabtu*	I wrote
3 m.du.	*katabā*	they (two men) wrote
3 f.du.	*katabatā*	they (two women) wrote
2 m/f.du.	*katabtumā*	you (two) wrote
3 m.pl.	*katabū*	they (men) wrote
3 f.pl.	*katabna*	they (women) wrote
2 m.pl.	*katabtum*	you (men) wrote
2 f.pl.	*katabtunna*	you (women) wrote
1 m/f.pl.	*katabnā*	we wrote

But even this is simple compared with some languages. In
Fijian the system of pronouns makes the distinction between
singular, dual, 'little plural' and 'big plural'. In Tigre too
(Ethiopic) we find three forms of the noun e.g.:

färäs	a horse
'äfras	horses
'äfresam	a few horses

But this is not strictly the grammatical category of number, as
Tigre has many other forms too – not only 'little plurals' but even
'pejorative plurals' and 'diminutives', e.g. *gäzirät* 'an island' but
gäzeram 'some poor islands', *gäzirätit* 'a little island'. These
forms do not differ in any regular way in terms of number concord; most of them are singular, plural concord being restricted
almost entirely to plural forms of animate nouns. Concord in
terms of gender, however, is more relevant; oddly enough, it
might seem, *gäzeram* is masculine and *gäzirätit* is feminine. We
must perhaps treat these forms within derivation rather than inflection (see p. 57) and consider them to be on the 'edge' of

grammar, not involved directly in a grammatical category of the morphosyntactic kind.

PERSON is probably the one linguistic category that has clearly defined reference to non-linguistic entities. In traditional terms first person refers to the person speaking, second person to the person spoken to, and third person to the person (or thing) spoken about. Like gender and number, person often involves features of concord, especially with the verb, and in many languages, e.g. the Semitic languages, all three categories are involved in the paradigms of the verb, as we have seen already (p. 88). In languages with little or no inflection, however, we can recognize the category of person in terms of the pronoun, the words for *I*, *you*, *he*, etc. alone. Person thus differs in two major respects from gender. First, provided we take pronouns into account, it is almost certainly a universal feature. Secondly, it is dependent to a large degree upon the meaning of the category; we should not recognize person unless there was reference to speaker, person spoken to, etc. In this respect it contrasts with gender where the justification for the category (see on Swahili, p. 86) is almost wholly formal.

The definitions work well enough in the singular – a speaker, someone spoken to, someone spoken of. But in the plural it is more complex. Strictly, one might suppose, first person plural (*we*) ought to refer to a plurality of speakers, second person plural (*you*) to a plurality of people addressed and third person plural (*they*) to a pluraltity of people spoken of. But this is not so. The use of *we* to refer to a number of joint speakers is rare and is confined to 'choruses'. Choruses, in this sense, are not restricted to musical works or to drama (e.g. Greek comedies and tragedies); there are other kinds of chorus, e.g. the football crowd that yells 'We want four' after the third goal has been scored. Similarly, *you* does not refer only to people spoken to; it often refers to the person or persons spoken to plus others. *They* alone is restricted to our 'ideal' use; it refers solely to people spoken about. In terms of the singular pronouns the possibilities of interpretation for *we*, *you* and *they* are (with the dots to indicate that there is no upper limit of the possible numbers of 'I', 'you' or 'he' and that gender is being ignored):

we	I and I (and I . . .)
	I (and I . . .) and you (and you . . .)
	I (and I . . .) and he (and he . . .)
you	you and you (and you . . .)
	you (and you . . .) and he (and he . . .)
they	he and he (and he . . .)

Another, and perhaps simpler, way of stating this is to say that *we* means any group of people that includes the speaker, *you* any group that includes the person spoken to, except a group covered by *we*, and *they* any group not covered by *we* or *you*. There is a clear ordering of choice: use *we* if you can, *you* as a second choice and *they* as the final choice. In other words, *we* can include a person spoken to or a person spoken about, *you* a person spoken about but not the person speaking and *they* neither the person speaking nor the person spoken to.

Some languages make distinctions not found in English. A common one is between an 'exclusive' and an 'inclusive' *we*, the first standing for *you and he* (*they*) and the second for *you and I*. Although English does not have any formal mark of this distinction it is often clearly implied. For instance, the choice of *shall* or *will* is to some degree determined by this. The most likely interpretation of *If things get worse we shall act* and *If things get worse we'll act* is that in the first *we* is 'I and he or they', in the second it is 'I and you'.

There is a still more striking complexity: person (or person together with number) is often used in what seems to be a quite inconsistent way. For instance, although we can establish a second person singular form in a language it often turns out that the form is used only for a very restricted category of persons spoken to. If we consider English *thou* and *thee*, for instance, we find that apart from the use of these forms in dialects, they are used only to address God! He is the only 'person spoken to' for whom they are appropriate. In French and Italian similar forms are used only for addressing friends, equals and close relatives.

In France *tutoyer*, to use *tu* and *te*, means to address familiarly. In Italy a student addressing another student would be expected to use *tu* and *te*, but not if addressing his professor! But what are the alternatives? There seem to be two common ones. One is to use the plural form, which is what English and French have done – English *you*, French *vous* – though in English the *thou*, *thee* forms are so rare that it is almost certainly best to say that today *you* is both singular and plural. Another is to use the third person instead of the second plural, as Italian has done with *Lei* and *Loro* (*Lei*, moreover, is feminine – 'literally' *she*), though the distinction is made in the writing by using capital letters for the 'second person' use. German combines both conventions. It uses the third person plural form of the pronoun instead of both the singular and the plural second person polite forms, though again using a capital initial (*Sie* as in *Sprechen Sie Deutsch?* 'Do you speak German?'). Of course, what often happens, as has happened in English, is that the distinction between second person singular and plural eventually becomes completely lost. Not surprisingly, there are dialects of English where it has been recreated, e.g. in the South of the United States, where *y'all* (*you all*) is the plural form, *you* being restricted to the singular.

There are other eccentric usages: the royal or editorial *we* and, the matronly *we* of *How are we this morning? You* is very common as the indefinite unspecified pronoun, though it used to be frowned upon in school, and schoolboys were recommended to use *one* instead. As we saw earlier (p. 21) *they* is often used for singular reference where sex is unspecified, e.g. *If anyone comes, they can't get in*.

The pronoun system of some languages, especially of Southeast Asia, is much more complex, since whole sets of different forms are used according to the relative rank of the speakers and people spoken to. There are what are called 'honorifics', which are sometimes reflected in mock translation of, for instance, Japanese by the use of the word *Honourable*. This system is still within the grammatical category of person though its reference includes much more than the simple distinction of person(s) speaking, person(s) spoken to and person(s) spoken about.

With TENSE we move to consider a category associated directly with the verb. We have seen already that tense is often, though very misleadingly, associated with time, and the problem of tense in English is dealt with in some detail in Appendix C. There are few, if any, languages in which there is a category that is totally related to time, though there are some, e.g. Latin where a division into present, past and future is justified on formal grounds with some fairly clear relationship to time, e.g. *amo* 'I love', *amabo* 'I shall love', *amabam* 'I loved'; but even here *amabam* is perhaps better translated as 'I was loving' with *amavi* as the 'I loved' form. There is also the further complication that Latin has a set of 'perfect' forms with the same three tenses, *amavi* 'I have loved', *amavero* 'I shall have loved' and *amaveram* 'I had loved', and we must note that *amavi* occurs here too! Clearly Latin is a fairly complex language. Once we look at other languages many other non-correspondences between tense and time come to light. In Bilin (Ethiopian Cushitic) there are many different paradigms of the verb, translated not only by e.g. 'I, see', 'I saw', 'I shall see', etc., but also 'if I see', 'that I saw', 'who sees', etc. These fall very clearly into two main groups on formal grounds – the tonal features and certain vowel qualities involving vowel harmony (see pp. 46–7). These two groups are easily characterized as 'past' and 'present' tenses respectively, so that we find pairs differing only in tense (with these very clear features of tone and vowel quality) that would translate 'that I saw' and 'that I see' or '(I) who saw' and '(I) who see' as well as 'I saw' and 'I see'. But we then find two quite remarkable divergences between tense and time. Surprisingly all those that translate any kind of future 'I shall see', 'I should see', etc., are, in terms of the formal features, past tense. More disquieting, perhaps, the 'verb *to be*' is formed from two different verbs, one providing all the past tense forms, the other all the present tense forms; but the one that provides all the present tenses has the meaning associated with past tense and the one that provides the past tenses has the meaning associated with present tense! For this one verb (or strictly two verbs) the usual pattern of form and meaning is totally reversed. To put the situation paradoxically, the present tenses are all past and the past tenses are all present.

In many languages there is what is called 'aspect' as well as, or instead of, tense, tense supposedly referring to time and aspect to completion, duration and similar concepts. In Latin, we can treat the distinction between the perfect tenses and the others as one of aspect. In the Slavonic languages a regular distinction is made between verbs referring to completed and those denoting non-completed action; Russian has to distinguish between reading a book but not finishing it (*čitat'*) and reading a book and finishing it (*pročitat'*). In Classical Arabic the ONLY distinction in the verb seems to be one of aspect, complete and incomplete. But if we accept that we can never in formal terms establish tense simply in terms of time, the essential distinction between tense and aspect is lost. It is therefore unwise to talk of aspect, except where a language clearly has two separate verbal categories, as for instance Latin (and, perhaps, English), since we then need two names for two different formal categories; but we certainly do not maintain that there are in general two different categories clearly distinguished by their meaning.

The same remarks apply also to MOOD. In Latin and the Romance languages there is the subjunctive mood as well as the indicative (and the imperative), while Greek has the optative as well. In so far as the distinction of mood merely marks another dimension for the classification in formal terms of the verb forms, it is entirely satisfactory. In Latin we can classify them in three ways independently, in terms of tense, aspect and mood:

NON-PERFECT	INDICATIVE	SUBJUNCTIVE
present	*amo*	*amem*
future	*amabo*	—
past	*amabam*	*amarem*

PERFECT		
present	*amavi*	*amaverim*
future	*amavero*	—
past	*amaveram*	*amavissem*

(The grammar books, however, usually fail to make the non-perfect/perfect distinction so explicit in their exposition.)

The most common function of mood in Latin and Greek and other languages is its use in subordinate clauses. In Latin, for instance, the subjunctive is used for 'indirect commands', for purpose ('in order to . . .'), for clauses within reported speech, etc., while in Spanish there is a very complex system using subjunctives for the conditional clauses (those with 'if . . .'). In these, mood cannot be said to have any meaning; its use is determined quite automatically. Yet the Greek subjunctive was used in Homer for simple future time reference and the optative for vague possibility. To look for some 'real', universal, distinction between mood and tense, or mood, aspect and tense is almost certainly pointless. We shall find that their meanings refer to time, to possibility, to completion, etc., but seldom will there be any one-to-one relation between such meanings and the formal categories. We should be particularly careful not to take the formal categories of Latin, assign them generalized meanings and then impose them, mainly on the basis of those meanings, upon other languages.

Finally, VOICE raises a few interesting problems. Many languages show a difference between active and passive with the object of the active being the subject of the passive in such pairs of sentences as *John saw Bill* and *Bill was seen by John*. This raises some very important theoretical problems that we shall discuss later, because, unlike tense and mood, voice involves a change in the position and the function of other words in the sentence.

Again, not perhaps surprisingly, we often find more than the two distinctions of active and passive. Greek had a third, the middle, whose meaning was generally that of doing something for oneself or to oneself. A more complex, but wholly neat pattern is found in the Semitic languages. Consider, for instance, these forms of Tigrinya:

active	*qätäle*	he killed
passive	*täqätle*	he was killed
causative	*'aqtäle*	he caused to kill

| reciprocal | *täqatäle* | he killed and was killed |
| reciprocal-
causative
adjutative | *'aqqatäle* | he caused (them) to kill
each other
he helped to kill |

These are referred to by Semitic scholars as the 'derived' forms of the verb, but clearly if we do not confine voice to the European patterns of active and passive they are simply different voices of the Tigrinya verb.

In many languages, nevertheless, voice is concerned only with active and passive, and the most striking point is that the object of an active sentence is the subject of the passive as in our pair *John saw Bill* and *Bill was seen by John*. But there are some odd features even in English. Why do we say *The bells rang* and *The fabric washes easily*? For we also have active sentences with *the bells* and *the fabric* as the objects – *They rang the bells* and *She washed the fabric*. It would seem that in the first two sentences *rang* and *washes* are somehow passive in meaning, though still active in form. We could, perhaps, treat them as another mood in English, perhaps the English 'middle'; but that would be misleading because there is no distinct set of forms. It is rather that active forms of the verb often have a meaning in which the subject rather than the object is the 'goal', i.e. the recipient of the action instead of being the 'actor'. This is yet a further example of non-correspondence between formal categories and meaning.

Some scholars have pointed out the similarity of this feature of English to what is called the 'ergative' case of some languages (such as Basque and Hindi). In these the subject of an intransitive verb (one without an object) usually has the same case form as the object of a transitive verb. (This is strikingly different from the position in more familiar languages where the subjects of intransitive verbs are, like the subject of transitive verbs, in the nominative case while the object of the latter is in the accusative.) The case of the subject of the transitive verb in these languages is referred to as the 'ergative'. In Basque, for instance, 'the man has beaten the dog' is *gizonak jo du chakurra* while 'the man has come' is *gizona dator*. Here *chakurra* 'dog' in the first sentence and *gizona* 'man' in the second are in the same case while the *-ak* ending of *gizonak* marks it as 'ergative'. If we now consider again the English examples *They rang the bells* and *The bells rang* we see that the two occurrences of *the bells* have functions in terms of sentence structure (object in the first, subject in the second). Yet in more notional terms their function is the same. *The bells* is the 'goal' – they undergo the action – while *they* is the 'actor', the one who performs it. This function would be marked formally in Basque or any other 'ergative' language, while English marks instead (by sentence position) subject and object. But it is clear that in English subject does not equal actor; it can as in the second sentence equal goal instead.

I have left CASE until last because it is not a category in the same sense as the others. What we have in certain languages (Latin is a good example) is a set of forms of the noun, such as that for *amicus*, which is already given on p. 15. But this is a collection of forms that are not (necessarily) similar in function. The nominative and the accusative are markers of sentence function, of subject and object respectively; this is largely true too of the dative, which marks the indirect object. In contrast, the vocative has no function at all within the sentence, but it is the form used for addressing or calling, while the main function of the genitive is within the noun phrase, to indicate the possessor, as in *pueri liber* 'the boy's book'. The ablative is mainly used after prepositions such as *ex* and *ab* with a meaning of 'from'. But to complicate matters the accusative is also used with prepositions meaning 'to'. We can do no more, then, than set out the paradigm, i.e. list forms of the noun which have a whole variety of functions. Not surprisingly, in other languages there are cases with other names and other meanings, e.g. the allative for motion towards and the comitative to translate 'with', and we have already mentioned the ergative. Finnish is often quoted as the language with the most cases – nominative (subject), genitive ('of'), accusative (object), inessive ('in'), elative ('out of'), illative ('into'), adessive ('on'), ablative ('from'), allative ('to'), essive ('as'), partitive ('involving part of'), translative ('involving change to'), abessive ('without'), instructive ('by') and comitative ('with'). But although this is interesting, it is probably misleading. For most of these 'case forms' are no more than noun forms with 'post-positions', i.e. suffixes functioning like prepositions but occurring at the end of the word instead of preceding it.

English has very little in the way of case. We can, if we wish, talk about the possessive *'s* as the genitive in e.g. *John's*, or distinguish the pronouns *I/me, he/him*, etc., in terms of case, though not in terms of the Latin nominative and accusative, since they appear not only as objects but after all prepositions and even as 'subjects' in e.g. *Who's there? Me*. But there are two words of warning. First, we must not then import case into the nouns and say that *John* and *Bill* are in different cases in *John hit Bill*. Secondly, we must not look for yet another case for *me* in *He gave me a book*. This is not dative, for English has no dative, unless we simply impose the Latin case system upon English. But why that of Latin, why not that of Finnish, Basque or Chinese?

There is, however, an interesting speculative point. If we re-consider the sentence that we discussed in the section dealing with voice: *The fabric washes well*, we can compare this not only with *She washes the fabric*, but also with *Brand X washes whiter*. In other words the subject of *wash* can be not only the 'actor' (*She*) or the 'goal' (*the fabric*), but also the 'instrument' ('Brand X'). It has been suggested that we might look at these features in terms of 'case'. The point of this suggestion is that it takes account of the fact that such 'cases' are not formally marked in any uniform way and that we can (and should) look at the ways in which they are handled in English and other languages. This is an interesting piece of speculation, but it has nothing to do with grammatical case in our sense, beyond the fact that some of the distinctions we might need ('agent', 'object', 'instrument') are marked formally in some languages by case endings. But there will be more on this in 5.4.

2.6 Concord and government

In the first chapter we discussed the now traditional but rather unsatisfactory classification of languages into three types – inflected, agglutinative and isolating. The first two, inflected and agglutinative languages, share the characteristic that in both there are different forms of the same word (using 'word' in the sense we discussed on p. 52). It follows that in such languages there must often be choice between the forms of a word. Why do we have *likes* rather than *like* in English, *petite* rather than *petit* in French, *amamus* rather than *amatis* in Latin?

Sometimes the choice is free; for instance, we can choose between the present and the past tense forms of the verbs in the sentences:

> *The boy likes ice cream,*
> *The boy liked ice cream.*

These are of course different in meaning but the choice of *likes* and *liked* is not determined by anything in the sentence.

By contrast with the sentences above there is no freedom of choice between the forms of the verb in:

> *The boy likes ice cream,*
> *The boys like ice cream.*

Although we have again two forms of the verb LIKE, the choice is determined by the occurrence of *boy* and *boys*. (We might perhaps argue that there is freedom of choice between *like* and *likes* but that this choice then determines the choice of *boy* or *boys*. This raises a 'chicken and egg' problem that we shall not discuss here – what determines what?) What is important is that *boy* and *likes* occur together as do *boys* and *like*, and that if we pair them wrongly we shall produce a sentence that will be immediately recognized as 'ungrammatical'. We have here what is sometimes referred to as 'linkage', but it is better to consider it in terms of restriction (grammatical restriction), since the choice of the forms is restricted by grammatical considerations.

In the traditional grammars these restrictions are dealt with under two headings, concord (or agreement) and government. Both are very clearly exemplified in Latin; this is hardly surprising since their justification rests largely on the requirements of Latin grammar.

Let us first consider concord. In Latin a verb is said to agree with its subject (a noun or a pronoun) in person and number and an adjective is said to agree in number, gender and case with the noun it modifies. Agreement of the verb with its subject in number is shown by:

puer venit	the boy comes
pueri veniunt	the boys come

The singular noun form *puer* requires a singular verb form *venit*, while the plural *pueri* requires the plural *veniunt*, and the verb is said to agree in number, singular or plural, with the noun. Similarly, we may compare the second example above with:

nos venimus	we come
vos venitis	you (plural) come

The difference now is one of person – first person, second person or third person – and again the choice of the verb form depends on the subject (which in these two examples is a pronoun). The verb is said, then, to agree with the noun in person (as well as in number). There are similar examples in French, German, Italian, Spanish and other languages. In French, for example, we have:

le garçon vient	the boy comes
les garçons viennent	the boys come

In French, incidentally, though there are often five different forms for any one tense of the written language, there are frequently only three different forms in the spoken language, e.g.:

(*je*) *chante*	ʃᾶt	I sing
(*tu*) *chantes*	ʃᾶt	you sing
(*il*) *chante*	ʃᾶt	he sings
(*nous*) *chantons*	ʃᾶtɔ̃	we sing
(*vous*) *chantez*	ʃᾶte	you sing
(*ils*) *chantent*	ʃᾶt	they sing

Only the 'we' and 'you' forms differ from the rest.

In English there are two forms only: *comes* which occurs with *he*, *she*, *it* and all singular nouns, and *come* which occurs with all the other pronouns. Clearly there is still concord, but we surely do not need to talk about concord in terms of person as well as number. We do not, that is to say, want to make all the distinctions of first, second and third person as well as singular and plural, when there are only two possible forms of the verb. The fact is simply that there is one form for the third person singular and another for the rest. We should be wise to hesitate before setting up such a complex system to deal with just two forms.

To illustrate in full the agreement of adjectives with nouns in Latin we should need to write out the whole number, gender and case paradigm to produce thirty-six ($2 \times 3 \times 6$) forms in all. But a brief illustration can be provided by taking one adjective-noun sequence and contrasting it with three other such sequences differing each in number, gender and case respectively:

vir bonus	a good man
viri boni	good men (number: plural)
mulier bona	a good woman (gender: feminine)
viro bono	to a good man (case: dative)

The situation in German and Russian is similar to that in Latin, though there are fewer cases in German. In the Romance languages there are no cases, but there is agreement in number and gender, as in Italian:

il uomo buono	a good man
gli uomini buoni	good men
la donna buona	the good lady
le donne buone	the good ladies

In French the pattern is clear only in the written language, for in the spoken language many of the contrasts are lost (see p. 33). It should be noted too that in the Italian examples the articles are also involved in the agreement. This is also true of French, Spanish and German, and in German it is a matter of case as well as number and gender:

der gute Mann	the good man
des guten Mannes	of the good man (genitive)

Nothing similar exists in English.

Let us now turn to government. In Latin, prepositions and verbs are said to govern nouns in a certain case. Thus *a* ('from') governs nouns in the ablative while *ad* ('to') governs nouns in the accusative:

a monte	from the mountain
ad montem	to the mountain

Similarly, some verbs govern the objects in the accusative, others in the genitive, others in the dative and still others in the ablative:

hominem videre	to see a man (accusative)
hominis memini	to remember a man (genitive)
homini parere	to obey a man (dative)
gladio uti	to use a sword (ablative)

In languages such as English and French it is doubtful whether this concept of government can be usefully applied. Case can be established only for the pronouns and then only a system of two cases, nominative and accusative – *I/me, he/him, we/us, je/me, il/le*, etc. But the distinction does not depend on the verb, since there is no variation with different verbs, but only on the grammatical function of subject and object. The point is quite simply that with pronouns there is one form for the subject and another for the object. There is little value in talking about verbs governing their objects in the accusative if this is the ONLY case in which they govern nouns. There is, indeed, no more reason for talking about verbs governing their objects in the accusative than of verbs governing their subjects in the nominative (and this has been suggested), since the choice of case does not depend on the verb, but the function of the pronoun in the sentence. In French the position is slightly more complicated as there are three pronoun forms for some pronouns, e.g. *il/le/lui*, but again the choice does not depend on the verb but on the function of the pronoun.

As was suggested earlier, this whole dichotomy of agreement and government is a product of Latin grammar. Verbs and adjectives are said to agree with nouns, but nouns are said to be governed by prepositions and verbs. Why this distinction? Is it that where the noun is the determining factor we speak of agreement, where its form is determined we speak of government? This is not quite the answer. In the examples of government it is clear that we have the FORM of a noun determined by a particular verb or class of verb (not a form of a verb). Thus the verb PAREO 'obey' (in all its forms) takes the dative, i.e. requires a dative form of a noun. On the other hand, where there is agreement in number and case between adjective and noun we find that one form of a noun requires the corresponding form (i.e. with the same number and case) of an adjective:

vir bonus   a good man (both nominative singular)
viros bonos   good men (both accusative plural)

We have a clear distinction, then, between two kinds of linkage: (1) of a word or class of word requiring a particular form of another word and (2) a form of one word requiring a corresponding form of another. The labels 'government' and 'agreement' would seem to be applicable to these two situations respectively, but this will involve some modification of traditional practice. For instance, it is usually said that French adjectives agree with nouns in number and gender as in:

le bon garçon	the good boy
les bons garçons	the good boys
la bonne fille	the good girl
les bonnes filles	the good girls

There is clearly agreement in number in our sense; a particular form of the noun requires a particular form of the adjective – both forms must be either singular or plural. But with gender this is not so. It is a word, the lexical item for 'boy' or for 'girl', and not any particular form of the word, that requires a particular form of the adjective, either masculine or feminine. But this is not agreement on our definition, but government. We ought to say, then, that in French, nouns govern the adjectives for gender.

Often government and agreement (in our precise sense) are involved in the linkage of identical items. An example would be the Latin:

viro bono paruit.   He obeyed the good man.

Here we must say that:

(1) the verb (*paruit*) governs the noun (*viro*) in case (dative).
(2) the adjective (*bono*) agrees with the noun in case.
(3) the adjective also agrees with the noun in number (singular).
(4) the noun governs the adjective in gender (masculine).

This may seem complicated because to account for the number and case of *bono* we have to talk about agreement with the noun (whose case is determined by government by the verb), while the gender of the adjective is determined by government by the noun. No wonder, one may think, traditional grammar did not use the terms government and agreement in this way. But the distinction is important because government in our sense involves the lexicon while agreement does not: if a particular verb requires a particular case, or a particular noun requires a certain gender form of the adjective, this has to be indicated in the dictionary. We have to show that Latin PAREO takes the dative or that French TABLE requires *la* and not *le*, or *petite* and not *petit*. Inconsistently, the dictionaries talk about TABLE being feminine but do not talk about PAREO being dative, though the position is exactly the same; in both instances the characterization of the class of noun or verb to which they belong is that they require a particular form of another word somewhere in the sentence.

What happens in Latin is not, of course, typical of all other languages. We find different grammatical categories involved in what seem to be conditions similar to those of Latin or the European languages. For instance, we have noted that the verb agrees with the noun-subject in number, with further (and more complex) relations with pronouns in terms of person. In many languages, however, gender as well as number and person is involved in the relations between the noun and the verb. This is particularly true of the Semitic and Cushitic languages (see p. 88). A feminine noun will be accompanied by a feminine form of the verb. Moreover, the second and third person pronouns are distinguished for gender and also require appropriate forms of the verb. Oddly enough, the first person pronouns are not so distinguished; apparently there is less need to indicate gender when referring to oneself. It has been suggested that gender is a concord feature even in French, in its spoken form at least, as in:

> *le garçon travaille-t-il?*
> *la jeune fille travaille-t-elle?*

For we could quite reasonably regard the pronoun here as part of the verb (or its suffix). On that interpretation we have here an example of the noun governing the verb in gender.

In the Semitic languages the verbs often have two kinds of endings, one relating to the subject, the other to the object, so that they can be simultaneously governed by or agree with two different nouns, the subject and the object. In the examples below we illustrate government in gender by both subject and object in Tigrinya:

(Subject)	(Object)	(Verb)	
säb'äy	*nəsäb'äy*	*qätiluwo*	the man killed the man
säb'äy	*nəsäbäyti*	*qätiluwa*	the man killed the woman
säbäyti	*nəsäb'äy*	*qätilätto*	the woman killed the man
säbäyti	*nəsäbäyti*	*qätilätta*	the woman killed the woman

Further examples would show agreement of the verb with both subject and object in number. The forms of the verb with plural subjects and objects would be *qätilomwom, qätilomwän, qatilänom, qatilän'än*.

Sometimes it is not the category involved that is strange by European standards, but the grammatical construction. In some languages, for instance, there is government in the possessor/ possessed (genitive) construction of the kind exemplified by *the boy's book*. We have already seen what happens in Bilin (see p. 70). In effect, a genitive form in Bilin is treated exactly as though it were an adjective, and is declined like one. It is, therefore, governed by the noun in gender and agrees with it in case and number. It is worth noting perhaps that some traditional grammars of Latin suggested that the genitive was par excellence the adjectival case.

The Bilin example follows the European pattern, although it

involves a new kind of government and concord, in that it is the possessor which is marked: the word for 'man's' is the form in the 'genitive', as it would seem to be in English and as it certainly is in Latin. In some languages, however, it is the possessed noun that carries the mark to indicate the construction. It is as if in English we said *The boy book-his*. If this were, in fact, the English form, *his* would exhibit government in gender and agreement in number with the noun *boy*. A real example is to be found in Memomini, an Amerindian language, where 'that man's dog' is represented by *enoh enɛ·wih oti·hsɛhsan* but 'those men's dogs' is *akohenɛ· niwak oti·hsehsowa·wan*. The last words are the words for 'dog' or rather for 'dog-his' and 'dog-their'. The form of these depends on the number of the preceding noun, the possessor, for the possessor noun governs the possessed noun in number.

It is clear from previous chapters that the grammatical categories that are involved in government and agreement have very little exact meaning. What, then, is the function of government and agreement? What information do they provide? One answer is that they often provide little or no information and are almost completely redundant. French would be no less intelligible, and would certainly be easier to learn, if we did not have to bother with the gender and the number of adjectives, if in fact its adjectives followed the same pattern as those of English. For although the gender and number of an adjective is an indication of the structure to which it belongs (an adjective is thus identified as modifying a certain noun), this relationship is already indicated by the position of the adjective – i.e. before or after the noun. We do not therefore need its gender and number to establish that relationship. Thus, in languages where there is a fairly fixed order of words, and where that order indicates the grammatical relations between the words, concord and government would appear to be unnecessary luxuries (or difficulties). By contrast, in Latin, and especially Latin verse, the order of the words is not fixed and the concord-government patterns are all-important in establishing the grammatical structure. In Virgil for instance we find (the opening words of the *Eclogues*):

> *Tityre tu patulae recubans sub tegmine fagi*
> *silvestrem tenui musam meditaris avenae.*

But this cannot be understood unless we note that *patulae* goes with *fagi*, *silvestrem* with *musam* and *tenui* with *avenae*. That they do is clear from their number, gender and case.

This of course explains why number is not directly associated with counting or gender with sex. Part of the function of these categories (sometimes the major part of their function) is to indicate syntactic relations – that an adjective and a noun together form a single phrase or that a noun is the subject or object of a verb. Where such functions are clearly marked in other ways these categories become redundant and are often lost, as gender has been lost in English.

3. 'Structural' Linguistics

For many years, from at least the early nineteen-thirties until the late nineteen-fifties, the most influential school of linguistics was one which is usually described as 'structural' and associated chiefly with the name of the American linguist, Leonard Bloomfield. There were other important American linguists before or contemporary with Bloomfield, notably Franz Boas and Edward Sapir, but Bloomfield's influence was paramount in this period.

As its name suggests, the main thesis of this school was that language had a structure. But in itself this word 'structure' does not mean very much. In one sense all linguists are, or ought to be, structuralist in that they are looking for 'regularities', 'patterns' or 'rules' (I use quotation marks because all of them probably mean the same thing though different schools insist on one rather than the other). But Bloomfieldian, or 'post-Bloomfieldian' linguistics (for structuralism belongs to Bloomfield's followers rather than Bloomfield himself), envisaged language structure in a very precise and limited way. In particular it was associated with the 'phoneme' as the unit of phonology (the sound system) and the 'morpheme' as the unit of grammar. Phonemes are the sounds or strictly the distinctive sounds of language – *cat* consists of the phonemes /k/, /æ/ and /t/, *tough* of the phonemes /t/, /ʌ/ and /f/; an explanation of the morpheme is to come. These are both units of form, not of meaning, though there was considerable controversy among linguists about the question as to whether morphemes should or should not be considered as having meaning. The essential sense, however, in which the approach is structuralist is that the language is supposed to be actually composed of morphemes in sequence, i.e. of 'strings' of morphemes and similarly, though at a different level, of strings of phonemes.

Morphemes in general are larger than phonemes; in fact they are composed of phonemes, it being a requirement that a morpheme must consist of one or more phonemes. Thus *singing* would be said to be made up of the phonemes /s/, /i/, /ŋ/, /i/ and /ŋ/ and of the morphemes *sing-* (or /siŋ/) and *-ing* (or /iŋ/). To establish this morphemic and phonemic structure the linguist must establish first of all what the morphemes and phonemes of the language are by segmenting and classifying actual language material, and then must see clearly what combination of units of the same kind may occur (this is known as 'tactics') and how the morphemes are made up of phonemes. It was recognized that there must be units larger than the morpheme, though these were never very clearly defined (see p. 124). But here again the same principles would apply; language would actually consist of such units and it was the task of the linguist to establish what they were and how they related to one another and to the other (smaller) units of the language.

Bloomfield's interest in this type of approach stemmed from his desire to be completely empirical and scientific. In particular it is to be associated with the extreme 'mechanistic' point of view that he maintained. He strongly opposed the 'mentalists' who accounted for human conduct, and speech in particular, in terms of a non-physical '*spirit*, or *will* or *mind*'. He maintained that the variability of human behaviour is due only to the great complexity of the human body and in particular of the nervous system and he held that all human activity could be described in purely scientific terms. This led him to some conclusions and assumptions that cannot in fact be maintained. He argued, for instance, that we can define a word like *salt* precisely because we can give it a scientific definition (sodium chloride or NaCl), but that for other words like *love* and *hate* we simply lack the necessary knowledge (with the implication that they could be accurately defined if we had that knowledge). But the real truth is that almost all words are like *love* and *hate*, and that even *salt* is not strictly definable in scientific terms. It is rather that the scientist has used everyday terms and then made them more precise for his own purpose, but that does not invalidate the everyman's use of the word. Salt is the stuff we put on our food, with a salty taste. If the chemist tells us how it is usually made up, that does not alter the meaning of the word for us, for salt was salt before any chemist ever analysed it. Bloomfield's error can perhaps be seen more clearly if we try (as we can) to give a scientific definition to words like *mass* and *force*, for here clearly the physicist's use of these terms is not the same as that of the man-in-the-street and again the former is ultimately derived from the latter rather than vice versa.

Bloomfield also thought that phonemes, the sounds of the language, could be defined in purely physical terms. In 1934 he prophesied that 'within the next decade' the phonemes of languages would be defined in the laboratory by their physical characteristics. Sadly, this has proved to be false. It is because it is false that there has been no simple machine that will simply convert speech into written symbols. The automatic typewriter that can take dictation is still a long way from perfection. The reason is that the various sounds of language do not, paradoxically perhaps, have their own individual physical characteristics; they not only vary greatly from one context to another but are not even completely separate in the stream of speech. The fact that we can hear *cat* as /k/, /æ/ and /t/ (three phonemes) is due to a very large degree to the fact that we (as hearers) interpret a very complex set of sounds in this way and not to the fact that there are three clearly definable sounds in sequence.

Some of Bloomfield's successors went much further than he did in their attempts to make their linguistics scientific. They postulated not only that language has a phonemic-morphemic structure but also that the structure can and must be discovered by a set of rigorously defined procedures. In particular they required that there should be a strict order of discovery. First we must find the phonemes, and then the morphemes, each without any reference to anything that had not already been empirically established. This meant not only that the phonemes had to be found without reference to the grammar (the morphemes), but that both had to be discovered without reference to semantics (meaning). One linguist indeed suggested that in theory it would be possible for the phonemes of a language to be discovered from a set of tape recordings without any knowledge of what the language material meant. In a similar fashion the morpheme could be discovered from the phonemes by simply looking for recurrent sequences of phonemes. The curious thing was, however, that no linguist ever tried to do this in actual practice. These were theoretical ideals; the phonemes and morphemes had to be established AS IF these theoretical ideals were put into practice. But in fact linguists DID make use of the meaning of the words in establishing the phonology and the grammar, and of their knowledge of the grammar in establishing the phonology. In retrospect today this extreme theoretical viewpoint seems almost incredible. Why should it be a virtue not to make use of one's knowledge of other areas of the language? Would we not rather expect there to be total interdependence of all the levels of analysis? The cause of this perverse approach was almost entirely reaction against notional grammar of the traditional kind. The vagueness of the notions employed, and the lack of any serious attempt to provide explicit statements of the criteria were, rightly, anathema to the linguists of the time. But it should not have to follow that because meaning was used in a very cavalier and often irrelevant way in the establishment of the grammatical categories it should be totally excluded. Giving ample recognition to form does not exclude the possibility of recognizing meaning also (see p. 40). But this excessive concentration on methods of discovery was (and still is for some) a vital part of structural linguistics.

3.1 Morphemes

For reasons that we discussed in the previous chapter, many linguists, particularly in America, came to the conclusion that the word was not, or at least not necessarily, the basic unit of grammar, but that often we have to look to something smaller than the word. Writing in his book *Language*, published in 1921, Edward Sapir suggested that the 'true, significant elements of language' were 'words, significant parts of words, or word groupings'. He suggested moreover that the words *sing*, *sings* and *singer* should all be analysed as 'binary expressions', i.e. composed of two parts.

This idea is stated more clearly by Leonard Bloomfield in the book that was also entitled *Language* and first published in 1933 (though Bloomfield had set out his ideas earlier in articles written for professional journals). He pointed out that there were linguistic forms which were never heard in isolation (and so were not words by his definition); these he called *bound* forms. His examples were the *-y* (/i/) of Johnny and Billy and the *-ing* (/iŋ/) of *singing* and *dancing*. These were clearly linguistic forms since they 'are phonetic forms . . . with constant meaning'.

Bloomfield went on to define the smallest forms of this kind as morphemes. His precise definition of a morpheme is 'a linguistic form that bears no partial phonetic-semantic resemblance to any other form'. This rather forbidding negative definition is in reality quite simple. By 'bears no partial . . . resemblance' he meant that no part of it had any resemblance. To obtain the morphemes, then, we must divide up our linguistic forms until no part of any one is similar to any other in its phonetic and semantic characteristics. Thus *dancing* cannot be a morpheme because part of it resembles the first part of *dances* and part of it resembles the second part of *singing*. But if we divide *dancing* into two – *danc-* (/dæns/) and *ing* (/iŋ/) – these forms have no partial resemblance to any other forms and, therefore, are morphemes.

At first sight the usefulness of the concept of the morpheme is obvious. We can treat *singing* and *dancing* each as two morphemes but with an identical second morpheme *-ing*, and we can similarly analyse *danced* and *loved* or *cats* and *bricks*. We must simply divide up the 'complex' forms of language until we arrive at these 'simple' forms (and Bloomfield used the term 'simple' for morphemes). The remaining task of the grammarian is simply to state all the possible combinations of these simple forms.

It is obvious that this kind of analysis works admirably for the agglutinative languages (see p. 55) and that any reasonable grammars of such languages should be along these lines. Our Swahili example *alikuona* (p. 54) consists of the elements (i.e.

morphemes) *a*, *li*, *ku* and *ona*. We may well ask, however, whether such an approach is suitable for the inflectional languages. Is it not precisely because they do not lend themselves to this type of analysis that they differ from the agglutinative ones? In the Greek example we considered (see p. 55) *lusontai* can be divided into six morphemes but can *luo:*?

Bloomfield stated that morphemes consisted of phonemes; the morpheme *-ing*, for instance, consists of the phonemes /i/ and /ŋ/. This, according to his view, is an essential part of the whole theoretical approach, indeed of the linguistic structure itself, and the task of the linguist is to discover that structure – by first segmenting the stream of language and then grouping the segments into classes. The first segmentation and classification is at the level of phonology (the sound system), resulting in the discovery of the phonemes; the second is at the level of morphology, resulting in the discovery of the morphemes. This fairly simple concept of linguistic structure proved impossible to verify in fact and as a result Bloomfield's simple notion of the morpheme had to be altered. It is interesting and instructive to trace the steps in which it was modified until it was in effect changed out of all recognition. The reason for these changes was, basically, the point discussed in the previous paragraph, that the idea of morphemes with constant phonetic and semantic identity is fully appropriate only to the agglutinative languages. Morpheme analysis, therefore, is essentially an attempt to mould all languages (including those that are inflectional) into the form of the agglutinative ones. This becomes clear if we look in detail at the various modifications that had to be made to Bloomfield's original morpheme. Many of them Bloomfield had to make himself – even in *Language* it is not held to be strictly true that 'morphemes consist of phonemes':

(1) Bloomfield found it necessary to talk of 'alternants'. His example was that of the plural form in English which even when written with an *-s* nevertheless has three phonological shapes:

/iz/	in	*glasses*
/z/	in	*pens*

/s/   in   *books*

Other examples go to show that /iz/ appears after sibilants and affricates (*glasses, roses, dishes, garages, churches, bridges*); /z/ appears after all other voiced phonemes (*saws, boys, ribs, sleeves, pens, hills, cars*), and /s/ after all other voiceless phonemes (*books, cliffs*). There is a very similar situation with the past tense morpheme which has three phonological shapes /t/, /d/ and /id/ as in *liked*, *loved* and *hated* respectively (/id/ occurring only after /t/ and /d/). Alternants of this kind Bloomfield called 'phonetic alternants' because they 'can be described in terms of phonetic modification'. These alternations are 'regular' because they are regulated by a characteristic of the accompanying forms, and 'automatic' because this regulating characteristic is phonemic. Later linguists used the term 'allomorph' (or simply 'morph') to designate the alternants, reserving the term morpheme for the whole class of alternants. Thus the plural morpheme {s} (with braces to show that it is a morpheme) would be said to have the allomorphs /iz/, /z/ and /s/ (with slant lines to show that these allomorphs consist of phonemes). This kind of alternation, moreover, was described by them as 'phonologically determined alternation' since it is determined by the phonological characteristics of the environment.

We should perhaps not be surprised that morphemes should undergo 'phonetic modification' as Bloomfield called it. It is a very common characteristic of language that one sound seems to determine the nature of another. As another linguist, Kenneth Pike, put it: 'Sounds tend to be modified by their environments.' This happens even in agglutinative situations. In Swahili, for instance, the form *m* 'him' is replaced by *mw* before vowels:

$$a - li - m - penda \qquad \text{he loved him}$$
$$a - li - mw - ona \qquad \text{he saw him}$$

The introduction of the notion of alternants or allomorphs may seem, then, to be justified, but it carries one important consequence. We can no longer say that morphemes CONSIST of phonemes, but rather that the allomorphs or alternants consist of phonemes. However plausible this modification may be it radically changes the model.

(2) Bloomfield also noted that there are irregular alternants. His examples were the first part of

knife	/naif/	knives	/naiv-z/
mouth	/mauθ/	mouths	/mauð-z/
house	/haus/	houses	/hauz-iz/

These are irregular because the final consonant is voiceless in the singular form and voiced in the plural – /f/ 'changes' to /v/, /θ/ to /ð/, and /s/ to /z/. This does not occur with most of the other words that end in the same consonants; we must contrast *cliffs*, *myths* and *creases*. There are other words with plurals similar to *knives* and *mouths* (e.g. *wives*, *wreaths*), but *houses* is in this respect quite idiosyncratic: there is no other plural form in the English language which involves an /s/ – /z/ alternation with an /iz/ ending.

Bloomfield also noted the plural of *ox*, *oxen*, which he said was 'suppletive'. It is neither regular nor in any way conditioned by its environment. Later linguists referred to this kind of alternation as 'morphologically conditioned alternation' because it was conditioned by the occurrence of a particular preceding (or, where appropriate, following) morpheme, and not by any phonological feature. It should be noted, however, that phonological and morphological conditioning are not alternatives. Many morphemes are both morphologically and phonologically conditioned. Thus the occurrence of /iz/ is morphologically conditioned in that it occurs with *glass*, *horse*, *crease*, etc., but not with *ox*, and phonologically conditioned in terms of the preceding sibilant or affricate.

This kind of alternation, and in particular that of *ox/oxen*, is less easy to reconcile with Bloomfield's morpheme. Are we to say that /ən/ is the same morpheme as the other plural morphs /iz/, /z/ and /s/, or are these two different morphemes with the same function? Most scholars concluded that they were the same morpheme, but not only is this kind of morpheme not composed of phonemes, though its alternants may be, but also there is no simple explanation of the alternation as there is for the phonologically conditioned allomorphs.

(3) In view of the fact that the plural of *sheep* is identical with that of the singular form, and that the same is true for the spoken form of *postman* (/pousmən/, see p. 31), Bloomfield also talked about 'zero' alternants and later scholars of 'zero' allomorphs. It was thought reasonable that morphemes could have zero allomorphs, though with the condition that not all the allomorphs can be zero. This is an important condition since otherwise we would say that CAT has a zero allomorph in the singular. (In itself, this suggestion is not altogether ridiculous: we might say it has zero in the singular and *s* in the plural; but we have then established a morpheme (zero) where there is no linguistic form at all anywhere in the language since English never has a formal mark of the singular.) The notion of the zero allomorph in *sheep* and also in *hit* (past tense) is a very useful one, but once again we are moving away from Bloomfield's conception. A zero element cannot really be said to have 'no partial phonetic-semantic resemblance to any other form'.

(4) The converse of the zero allomorph or morph is what Charles Hockett called the 'empty morph'. Sometimes in a language we find some phonological material that seems to belong to no morpheme at all. Hockett's examples were taken from an American Indian language, and there are examples in a number of languages, but there is just one possible example in English that we might consider. The plural form of *child* is *children* – phonemically /tʃildrən/. It is reasonable to regard /tʃaild/ in the singular and /tʃild/ in the plural as allomorphs of the same morpheme, and it is equally reasonable to identify the /ən/ with the /ən/ of *oxen*. What then can we say of the /r/? It is an 'empty' morph, since it belongs to no morpheme at all. However useful, the empty morph again cannot easily be related to Bloomfield's morpheme.

(5) Bloomfield also had to consider the analysis of such forms as *geese*, *men*, *took*, *knew*, as compared with *goose*, *man*, *take* and *know*. These he treated in terms of 'substitution alternants'. The substitution of /iː/ in *geese* or of /e/ in *men* for /uː/ and /æ/

respectively is, he said, an alternant of the normal plural suffix. Bloomfield's suggestion reappears in the works of Zellig Harris who recognized for *took* (/tuk/) as compared with *take* (/teik/) the allomorph /u← ei/ or /ei ～ u/ – i.e. '/u/ replaces /ei/' or 'change /ei/ to /u/'. But it is immediately obvious that these are very strange allomorphs; an instruction to replace one item by another can hardly be regarded as in any sense consisting of phonemes.

(6) Charles Hockett had a different solution for the same problem – /tuk/ is a 'portmanteau' morph, one that belongs simultaneously to two morphemes – *take* and *ed*. This, of course, preserves the notion that morphemes consist of phonemes, but with the reservation that individual morphemes do not always consist of phonemes, but that two or more morphemes jointly may be said to consist of phonemes. This solution is more plausible in those cases where the morphemes also have other allomorphs that are not portmanteaux. We may compare /tuk/ with /lʌvd/ (*loved*) which is clearly divisible into /lʌv/ and /d/, and since /lʌvd/ is two morphemes, it can be argued that /tuk/ is too. But we can less plausibly apply a similar analysis to the *o* of Latin *amo*, and treat it as a portmanteau belonging to the five morphemes first person, singular, present, indicative, active, since none of these morphemes seem ever to have their own individual allomorph; the forms are always 'fused', always portmanteaux. If we permit this analysis the charge can fairly be laid that we are cheating, for the notion of the morpheme as a recognizable unit with a phonetic and semantic 'shape' can hardly be maintained, if ALL the forms are portmanteaux.

(7) Bloomfield also suggested that we might have 'minus' features. The best known example is in the French adjective. For many words the difference between the masculine and the feminine form is that the feminine has an extra consonant or consonants (see pp. 32–3). Some of Bloomfield's examples are:

plat	/pla/	'flat'	*platte*	/plat/
laid	/lɛ/	'ugly'	*laide*	/lɛd/
distinct	/distẽ/	'distinct'	*distincte*	/distẽkt/
long	/lõ/	'long'	*longue*	/lõg/

We should wish to say that the final /t/ of /plat/ is dropped or deleted in the masculine rather than say that /t/ is added to /pla/ to form the feminine, for the latter solution would involve us in setting up a motley collection of consonants to be added as allomorphs of the morpheme {feminine}. Since the consonant varies from word to word it is far easier to suppose that the feminine form is the basic form and that the masculine form loses its final consonant or consonants, than to treat the many different final consonants as marks of the feminine. The term 'subtractive' morph was used by Zellig Harris to describe this feature. A little reflection will show that this is a very strange concept indeed if we are thinking in Bloomfield's terms. How can subtraction or a minus feature be composed of phonemes? This concept did not in fact find favour with later linguists, most of whom felt that the only correct solution was to treat all the various final consonants as allomorphs of the feminine morpheme. In so doing, while they avoided the difficulties that the concept of minus or subtractive morphs must raise, they lost the simplicity that Bloomfield was seeking. It is, perhaps, surprising that they did not at this stage ask whether the problems were not created by themselves through their acceptance of Bloomfield's concept of the morpheme.

Within the various viewpoints we have been considering, a number of solutions are possible for the same linguistic form. For instance, at least six interpretations of the relation of *take* and *took* can be given:

(a) *Take* and *took* are different (single) morphemes. This is perhaps the only real solution as a strict interpretation of Bloomfield's original concept, but it loses the important generalization that these words are comparable to *bake* and *baked*; the latter must surely consist of *bake-* /beik/ and *-d* /d/. Moreover, is it true that *take* and *took* have 'no partial phonetic semantic resemblance'? Their initial and final consonants are the same.

(b) *Take* and *took* are each two morphemes, with the shared allomorph /t . . k/ and further allomorphs /ei/ and /u/. This has the great advantage of identifying the shared part of the two forms, the /t/ and /k/ within one morpheme, and so preserving

Bloomfield's notion of 'phonetic forms'. It is attractive, more-over, because a similar analysis seems essential in some languages, e.g. Arabic where the consonants form the 'roots' and the vowels are part of the purely grammatical elements. Thus in *kataba* 'he wrote', *kutiba* 'it was written', it would seem that k..t..b is the morpheme 'write'. But this solution again destroys the parallelism with *bake* and *baked* for the former is usually to be regarded as one morpheme and the latter as two, the first morpheme plus *d*.

(c) *Take* is one morpheme, *took* two; /tuk/ is a portmanteau morpheme.

(d) *Take* is one morpheme, *took* two; *took* consists of the morphs /teik/ and /u ← ei/.

(e) *Take* is one morpheme, *took* two; *took* consists of two morphs, /tuk/ which is an allomorph of {take} and zero (/ø/) which is an allomorph of {d}. This is perhaps the best solution within the theory since it retains the pattern of *bake*/*baked*: *baked* consists of two morphemes in sequence – first the morpheme {bake} and then the morpheme {d}. *Took* similarly on this analysis consists of two morphemes – {take} and {d}, but with allomorphs /tuk/ and /ø/. There is one curious point, however; /tuk/ is a morphologically conditioned allomorph occurring in the im-mediate environment of {d} which is here /ø/, /teik/ occurs where there is no following {d}. If we think how we can recognize the morphs we appear to be saying that /tuk/ occurs before zero, and /teik/ before nothing!

(f) *Take* is one morpheme and *took* two; *took* consists of /t..k/ which is an allomorph of *take* and /u/ which is an allo-morph of /d/ (the other allomorph of *take* being, in the singular form, /teik/). This seems one of the least plausible of all the solu-tions because it treats the vowels of the two forms in totally different ways.

We can set out the various solutions most clearly in a diagram. The proposed morphemes are shown in the orthography and the morphs in a phonemic script (within slant lines):

(a) *take*   *took*
    /teik/   /tuk/

(b)	*take present*	*take d*	
	/t..k/ /ei/	/t..k/ /u/	
(c)	*take*	*take d*	
	/teik/	/tuk/ (portmanteau)	
(d)	*take*	*take d*	
	/teik/	/teik/ /u ← ei/	
(e)	*take*	*take d*	
	/teik/	/tuk/ /ø/	
(f)	*take*	*take d*	
	/teik/	/t..k/ /u/	

Once we have established the morphemes of a language (if indeed we can in spite of all the difficulties we have been discussing) the next task is to state how they can be combined; this clearly is an essential part of the grammatical structure of the language. For this we may turn once again to Bloomfield. He stated that the grammar of a language consisted of the 'meaningful arrangements of the linguistic forms', i.e. the possible arrangements of the morphemes to provide meaningful language. Bloomfield suggested that there were four ways of arranging the morphemes; these were 'order', 'modulation', 'phonetic modification' and 'selection'. In actual fact only two of these are strict matters of arrangement – order and selection. But the other two also raise problems and we must look at them in some detail.

First let us consider Bloomfield's 'modulation'. By this he meant the use of what he called the 'secondary' phonemes – those of intonation and pitch. We can, for example, pronounce *John* with a falling or a rising pitch and we can also contrast the noun *convict* with the verb *convict* simply by use of a different stress. These features of stress and pitch raise some very difficult problems for two reasons. First they are, so to speak, over and above the phonemes, the vowels and consonants, and do not occur in the sequence of strings of sounds. This was Bloomfield's reason for calling them 'secondary' (later linguists referred to them as 'supra-segmental'). Secondly, it is far from easy to describe them accurately, in the sense that though we may recognize the difference between a falling pitch and a rising pitch it is by no means clear how many kinds of rising or falling pitches we need to note as linguistically significant. In purely physical terms there is no limit to the number of distinctions of pitch that can be made, but how many do we need for 'meaningful' language? The difficulty arises largely because we have no clear correlation of these features with contrasts of meaning. The point is perhaps made clear if we compare intonation with the vowel sounds of a language. Theoretically, there is no limit to the number of actual vowel sounds that could be made, but for one language, e.g. English, we need only a limited number of contrasts to distinguish *pit*, *pet*, *pat*, *pot*, *part*, etc.; unfortunately we cannot in a similar manner pick out a limited set of intonation tunes. In some languages, of course, the 'tone' languages, pitch can be handled with the same kind of rigour as the vowel qualities (see p. 56). If there are three tones, high, mid and low, these can be clearly identified because they contrast in the sense that they (and often they alone) distinguish words with different meanings; but even in tone languages there is often intonation 'over and above' tone, so that the problem remains even there. What can the linguist do about these features if he wants to analyse his language in terms of morphemes? One solution is to treat them in a quite different way, i.e. not to handle them in a morphemic solution at all. But this hardly seems satisfactory; they are features of language with both sound and meaning and ought therefore to have a place in the grammar. Another solution, of course, is to treat them as morphemes but with the recognition that they are not in the 'normal' sequence of segments; if they are morphemes, they are of a kind that never follow the others sequentially. Bloomfield's notion of modification is, one would suppose, essentially the first solution and as such really does not explain the grammatical status of these features, but it must be admitted quite frankly that attempts to handle them within the morphemic model have been far from satisfactory.

Next let us look at 'phonetic modification'. Bloomfield's examples included the way in which *do* is combined with *not* to produce *don't* with a different vowel for the first part and the loss of the vowel for *not*, and the way in which *run* is 'modi-fied' to *ran*. We have already seen a number of examples of alternants of this kind (the *s* of *cats*, *dogs*, *horses*, the forms *knife*, *knives*, etc.). This however is not, within morphemic theory, really a matter of the 'arrangement' of morphemes, but of the classification of the alternants (morphs, or allomorphs). We do not need to say that there is any phonetic modification in the case of these alternants, we merely have to say that they *are* alternants and list them. It is a problem of making a clear statement of the possible alternations. However, there is underlying this apparently simple point a very important theoretical problem which is at the basis of Bloomfield's thought. In a strict sense phonetic modification and alternants are contradictory. If *run* and *ran* are alternatives, it is unnecessary, perhaps even silly, to say that *run* is modified to form *ran*. But we CAN ask whether it is better simply to list alternatives or to treat one form or a set of forms as being derived from the other. Should we, that is to say, simply list *run* and *ran* as equal alternative forms or should we say that *ran* is formed from *run* by a change of vowel? A later linguist, Charles Hockett, gave the names IA (Item and Arrangement) and IP (Item and Process) to these different approaches. Ironically, although Bloomfield himself was thinking about IP in 'phonetic modification', since one form is 'changed' into another, his successors opted wholly for IA and even implied that this was Bloomfield's view. They argued that all we have is a set of identifiable forms, e.g. *take*, *took*, *taken*, and it is nonsense to say that some are derived from others by any kind of change. There is no change; they are just there. Indeed some argued that to talk about one form changing into another was to confuse the description of a language with its history. In historical times forms may change, but at any one time one form cannot be said to change into another.

Today, however, the 'process' approach has become popular once again for two reasons. First, in some cases, there is some plausibility in the notion of change. If we consider the form *cat's* and *dog's* which is the shortened form of *cat is* and *dog is* we find that, as with the plural forms *cats* and *dogs*, the first ends with an /s/ sound, a voiceless sound, while the latter ends with the voiced /z/. But *is* by itself ends in a /z/ (/iz/). Is it not then reasonable to say that the final voiceless consonant /s/ of *cat's* represents a change from the voiced /z/ of /iz/ under the influence of the voiceless final sound of *cat*? There are plenty of examples of 'motivated' change of this kind in languages. For instance, we have in English a prefix *un-*, meaning 'opposite of'. Phonemically this is, perhaps, to be regarded as /ʌn/ but in speech it often occurs as /ʌm/ in, for example, *unpick*, or /ʌŋ/ in, for example, *unkind* (though in more formal speech it might still be /ʌn/ even in these words). There is an obvious reason: the nasal consonant has the same position of articulation (bilabial and velar respectively) as the following consonant. Instead, therefore, of merely listing the alternative forms, is it not more informative to think of the prefix being modified phonetically/phonemically to be like the consonant, a process traditional grammarians knew as 'assimilation'?

A more important reason, however, for the preference of a 'process' approach is that it is much simpler. All we have to do is to write simple rules that 'convert' one form into another. No longer do we need to argue what are the morphemes of *took* (p. 117). We merely write a rule that changes the vowel of *take* into *took* when associated with past tense (and we can, moreover, write a general rule about such vowel changes that will include *shake/shook, forsake/forsook*). There is nothing wrong with changing /ei/ to /u/ in a 'process' approach. Often we need a sequence of such rules because one form seems to depend on another which itself depends on yet another. For instance, the form *spoken* is clearly to be derived not from *speak* but from *spoke* (though *taken*, in contrast, is to be derived directly from *take*). So we have rules *speak* → *spoke* → with the derivation *spoken* (as contrasted with the separate *take* → *took, take* → *taken*). It would be difficult to make this point clear except with a process type approach. If we just looked for the separate morphemes we could do no more than list the three forms for each verb. We could then not identify the *-en* part as the 'past participle', since what is important is that in one form (*spoken*) *-en* is added to the past tense form, but in the other it is added to the present tense form, so that for *spoken* the mark of the past participle is not only the -*en* but also the fact that it occurs with *spoke* and not *speak* (it is not *speaken on the analogy of *taken*). If, however, we say that *spoken* is formed from *spoke*, not *speak*, while *taken* is formed from *take* not *took*, the point is made quite clearly. But to talk about one form being formed from another is to use the idea of process, not simply of arrangement. Clearly there are advantages in this kind of approach.

Bloomfield's two other 'ways of arranging' the form were 'order' and 'selection'. On the simplest interpretation these two together say no more than that the grammatical structure consists of morphemes in sequence; we select morphemes and we place them in an order. But Bloomfield was saying a little more than that. First, he wanted to point out how important order was; *John hit Bill* is to be contrasted with *Bill hit John*, and the fact that a morpheme occurs in a particular place is often as important as the fact that a morpheme occurs at all. The order of the morphemes, that is to say, often has a function very like the occurrence of a particular morpheme. In English, for instance, the occurrence of *John* in the first position usually marks it as the subject, while in many languages, e.g. Latin, the subject is marked by the occurrence of particular form, the nominative. While, therefore, it is in a sense a tautology to say that one feature of arrangement is order – since if forms are arranged they have to be in an order – it is important to stress that order has specific grammatical function.

There is a similar point about selection, but a rather more subtle one. Of course, we must always select one form rather than another, but Bloomfield's point was that when the same form is selected in combination with other forms the resultant combinations often differ from one another. Thus *drink milk* is different from *fresh milk*, and as a result of this difference we can identify *drink* as a verb and *fresh* as an adjective. Similarly, *John* with an 'exclamatory final pitch' produces a call, but *run* with the same pitch produces a command. This too allows us to identify the 'form classes' of *John* and *Run* (noun and verb). What Bloomfield is saying, then, is that the morphemes belong to various 'form classes' and that there are possible combinations of such classes with resultant different constructions and meanings. It is not simply a matter of stringing morphemes together, even if we string them in a certain order. We have first to identify the classes and state which classes may combine with which. We shall then find that the combinations themselves have a variety of functions (see p. 132).

3.2 IC analysis

It is reported that one American linguist of the 1950s remarked that syntax was that part of linguistics that everyone hoped the other fellow would do. For although they had, apparently, succeeded in establishing the smallest unit of grammar, the linguists had little to offer towards the total analysis of the sentence. What other grammatical units are there and how are they all combined?

The structuralists' answer was in part to start dividing the sentence up into its 'Immediate Constituents' – or ICs for short. It will be remembered that a 'scientific' approach was one in which there was a systematic attempt to establish or to 'discover' the linguistic elements. But beyond the morpheme it was not at all clear that there were any clearly definable units, until we reached the sentence. The initial emphasis, as a result, was upon pure segmentation, simply dividing the sentence into its constituent elements without, at first, knowing what these elements were. The principle was that we take a sentence and cut it into two and then cut those parts into two and continue with this segmentation until we reach the smallest units, the morphemes. (In fact, occasionally it seems difficult, if not impossible, to divide into two, and in some cases division into three or more parts is allowed, but in general the division is binary.)

This is quite simply illustrated by the sentence *A young man with a paper followed the girl with a blue dress*. We can show the order of the segmentation by using one upright line for the first cut, two upright lines for the second and so on (reasons for choice of division are given below), and so arrive at:

A ||| young |||| man || with ||| a |||| paper | follow- |||
ed || the |||| girl ||| with |||| a ||||| blue |||||| dress.

Another, now more common, name for this kind of analysis is 'bracketing'; we use brackets as in algebra. This is, however, more difficult to read unless we actually number the brackets, though in fact it is unambiguous:

> (((A) ((young) (man))) ((with) ((a) (paper))))
> (((follow) (ed)) (((the) (girl)) ((with) ((a)
> ((blue) (dress)))))).

Quite the best method of display is to use the principle of the family tree, with the main branching showing the main division and so on. In fact, the terms 'tree diagram' and 'branching' have become technical terms in this kind of analysis. For our sentence the tree would be:

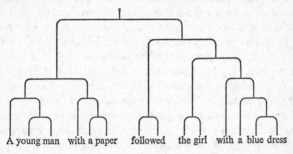

A young man   with a paper   followed   the girl   with a blue dress

How do we know where to make the cuts? The answer lies in the notion of 'expansion'. This is a technical term and is not to be taken in a literal sense. A sequence of morphemes that patterns like another sequence is said to be an expansion of it. The definition of expansion is, that is to say, in terms of similarity of pattern. We can test for this similarity by substituting one sequence for another, since to say that the sequence patterns are alike is to say that they will appear in the same kind of environment.

For IC analysis we are particularly interested in the substitution of longer sequences for shorter ones, and in particular for single morphemes. (It would seem that the term expansion is a little nearer its literal sense if one or two morphemes are 'expanded' into a larger number.)

In the sentence we have just been considering, the first ICs are

A young man with a paper and *followed the girl with a blue dress*. But why is this cut chosen rather than segmentation into *A young man with a paper followed* and *the girl with a blue dress*? The reasoning is as follows. First we can establish that *A young man with a paper* is an expansion of, say, *John*. That is to say, it patterns like *John* and can be substituted for *John*. We can see this from the fact that we can say *John followed the girl with a blue dress* or that we can say both *A young man with a paper came in* and *John came in*. Similarly, we can establish that *followed the girl with a blue dress* is an expansion of, say, *worked* since we can again substitute; we can say *A young man with a paper worked* or both *The boy followed the girl with a blue dress* and *The boy worked*. The second stage of the argument is to look at the sentence *John worked* and to argue that the obvious ICs are *John* and *worked* (the only other possible segmentation is into *John work-* and *-ed* since we have only three morphemes *John*, *work-*, and *-ed*). If we cut *John worked* into *John* and *worked*, it follows that because they are expansions of *John* and *worked* the ICs of our other sentence are *A young man with a paper* and *followed the girl with a blue dress*. We cannot segment into *A young man with a paper followed* and *the girl with a blue dress* because the first of these, at least, is not an expansion of any obvious smaller sequence (and in particular not of a single morpheme such as *John*).

Similar principles allow us to carry out IC analysis further. We can argue that *A young man* is an expansion of *children* and that *with a paper* is an expansion of *asleep* since they pattern in much the same way; comparison with *children asleep*, which has the IC analysis *children* and *asleep*, yields the ICs *A young man* and *with a paper*. To establish the division into *followed* and *the girl with a blue dress* we may take *hated* and *women* and the sequence *hated women*.

Expansion in this sense is not literally expansion; it is the technical name for the substitution of one sequence of morphemes for another. But there are examples in which we can think of expansion in terms of starting with one item and then successively adding items to it:

Children
American children
three American children
those three American children
those three American children with a dog

Though this is expansion in a more literal sense it is still expansion in the technical sense, for the last of these, *those three American children with a dog*, can be substituted for *children* in plenty of environments, e.g. *. . . like ice cream*. But many expansions are not of this kind. *With a paper* is an expansion of *asleep*, but it is not an expansion of any of its own parts, not of *with* or *a* or *paper*, since none of these can be substituted for it. The distinctions between these two kinds of expansion is not of great importance for the theory, but was handled in the literature in terms of 'endocentric' and 'exocentric' constructions, the endocentric ones being those in which there is expansion of the more literal kind. In endocentric constructions the element of which they are expansions (i.e. the element for which they can be substituted but which they also contain) was known as the HEAD; in our example the head is *children*. In exocentric constructions there is, by definition, no head.

It is obvious that in itself dividing a sentence into ICs does not provide much information. Nevertheless it can sometimes prove illuminating. It can sometimes account for ambiguities and distinguish them. A famous example is *old men and women*. Obviously we can see the ambiguity by paraphrasing; it is either *old men and women of all ages* or *old men and old women*. The principle of expansion here allows us two interpretations. Either *old men* is an expansion of a single morpheme (e.g. *men* or *boys*) or *men and women* is an expansion of a single morpheme (e.g. *people* or *men*). This would allow us to recognize two different IC analyses, as shown by the trees:

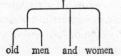
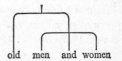

(There is a slight complication here – that with a conjunction such as *and* it is easiest to divide into three ICs instead of the usual two but we have noted that IC analysis is not always into two.) Similarly, we can make *Egyptian cotton shirt* unambiguous by having the first cut either after *Egyptian* (a cotton shirt made in Egypt) or after *cotton* (shirt made of Egyptian cotton). Slightly more difficult is *He said he was coming today*. If *today* 'belongs' with *said* the first cut is presumably after *coming*: if it 'belongs' with *coming* we shall make the first cut after *said*:

> *He said he was coming | today.*
> *He said | he was coming today.*

However, this is not enough. We must in some way be able to identify the elements into which we have cut the sentence. In the later literature a distinction is drawn between 'bracketing' and 'labelled bracketing', the first referring simply to the cutting of sentences into ICs, the second to their identification as subjects, objects, noun phrases, etc. We will consider labelled bracketing a little later on. Quite obviously it must be an essential part of any serious analysis. Mere cutting into ICs does not tell us very much. But in the traditional approach this cutting was fundamental and it is therefore appropriate to point out, at this stage, some of the difficulties it led to.

In the first place the cutting was supposed to precede any attempt to identify and classify, any attempt, that is, to label the ICs as subjects, objects, noun phrases, etc. This would be an essential part of the 'scientific' procedures of structuralism. In actual fact a great deal of IC cutting can be seen to be dependent upon prior assumptions about the grammatical status of the elements. The subsequent identification and classification, the 'labelling', thus involved circularity of argument. For instance, even when we start with a sentence such as *John worked* as the model for the analysis of *All the little children ran up the hill* we are assuming that both can be analysed in terms of the traditional categories of subject and predicate. This is implicit in the treatment of *All the little children* as an expansion of *John* and *ran up the hill* as an expansion of *worked*. There are many problems about the way in which the IC analysis should proceed that were solved only by tacit assumptions about the grammatical status of the elements. Far from the grammatical identification of the element being a result of the IC procedures, they were often a necessary prerequisite for any decision about cutting at all. For example, how should we cut *want to go*? There are two possibilities: *want / to go* and *want to / go*. If we compare it with *want food*, then clearly the first analysis must follow – *want / to go*. But if we compare it with *can go* then we must decide upon *want to / go*. Which is to be preferred? The answer given was in favour of *want / to go* because of the possibilities of *to go is easy* where obviously *to go* is a constituent. But why should this be thought relevant? We are in some ways identifying items that occur in quite different environments as being the same item and such identification is clearly grammatical. We are tacitly accepting an analysis which allows us to consider *to go* as some kind of nominal element, and favouring the comparison with *want food*, so that *to go* is an expansion of *food* because it is of the same grammatical type. A slightly different argument was used for *will be ready*. Is this *will / be ready* or *will be / ready*? We can compare *will want* to justify the first of these IC analyses and *was ready* to justify the second. It was argued that the second is correct because *will be* belongs to the same paradigm of the verb as *was* (one, presumably, being the future tense form of BE, the other the past tense form). But it is clear that in making the choice, we have assumed a great deal about English grammar.

A second difficulty is that a piece of language often cannot be cut into two because elements that belong together are separated in the sequence. This phenomenon is known as 'discontinuity'. For instance if we consider *the best team in the world* it is fairly obvious that *best* and *in the world* belong closely together and that the ICs (ignoring for this purpose the article *the*) are *team* and *best in the world*. But we cannot make a single cut to indicate this because one IC is already in two parts that are separated by the other. A very familiar type of discontinuity is provided by the so-called phrasal verbs, *make up*, *put down*, *take in*, etc., in for example:

> *She made the whole story up.*
> *The conjurer completely took the children in.*
> *The general soon put the rebellion down.*

With such verbs the adverb *up, in, down,* etc. may often follow
the object, as in these examples, yet it clearly belongs with the
verb as a single constituent. To take the first example we can first
cut into *She* and *made the whole story up,* but what then? The
only plausible solution is to recognize a division between *made . . .
up* and *the whole story.* There are plenty of other examples of discontinuity; another is *such a lovely house* where presumably we
must divide into *a* and *such . . . lovely house.* One of the most
important examples is provided by the question forms of the
type *Is John coming?* Here we must divide into *Is . . . coming* and
John. We cannot possibly show these as ICs by using brackets or
the upright lines. We can, if we wish, illustrate, by using the tree
diagram, but ONLY if we allow the branches to cross one another:

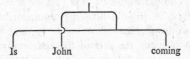

An alternative way would be to use boxes of the kind:

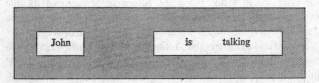

We can again show the discontinuous elements by shaping the
boxes:

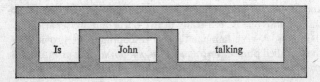

The objection to both these diagrams is that they are really 'dodges'. They do not strictly conform to the notion of cutting into elements at all. Of course we can always carry on IC analysis by merely permitting discontinuity, but this does surely make less plausible the very assumption on which IC analysis is based – that language is essentially a one-dimensional linear string which can be chopped up into decreasing segments. It must be recalled that IC analysis depends on expansion, the substitution of sequences of morphemes by other sequences and by single morphemes, but discontinuous elements are not sequences.

There is yet a third difficulty with IC analysis. It seems from the way in which it has been used that it is tacitly assumed that the ICs will usually be in terms of words, or at least that there will be no division into pieces smaller than words (morphemes) until all the words have been divided. This is clear to some degree from the fact that the longer sentences are regarded as expansions of two word sentences such as *John worked*. No one challenges the cut here as *John | worked* because that is the only division IF we divide first into words. But there are occasions where dividing first into words or groups of words will not work. Again there is a notorious example – *the King of England's hat* (cf. p. 45). Granted that *the King of England's* is a constituent (after cutting first between *England's* and *hat* and then between *the* and *King*) how do we now proceed? One might suggest *the King | of England's* but surely *the King of England's* is like *John's* where the cut must be *John | 's*. So here we must allow for *the King of England | 's*. But this is a little strange; one constituent consists of three words plus part of a word, the other of just part of a word. An even more intriguing problem is provided by the examples such as *criminal lawyer* quoted on p. 45. Perhaps we ought not to have any rules about dividing first into words, but if so, we may have lost the very test by which we have usually proceeded. For how otherwise do we know that we must divide *John worked* into *John | worked* and not *John work | ed*?

We can give an answer to this semi-rhetorical question by saying that *John worked* represents a familiar structure, that of subject and complement. In fact a great deal of IC analysis was based on decisions of this kind. But the point that I have been making is that such decisions ought according to the theory to have been made after the cuts and not to be implicit in the cutting itself. The picture then of first cutting and subsequently classifying the elements is basically a false one.

However, even if it were possible to make all the IC cuts without reference to our grammatical knowledge, cutting alone would not take us very far. IC analysis, therefore, always involved not merely cutting but also the identification of the elements in grammatical terms. There was not merely bracketing but labelled bracketing. This of course makes IC analysis much more 'powerful' (this too has become a semi-technical term). It can say much more about the structure of the sentences than mere cutting can.

Again, this can be illustrated by considering examples of ambiguity. A good example is provided by the joke '"Time flies". "You can't; they fly too fast."' There is only one IC analysis – *Time / flies*, but two different structures. In the intended sense we should wish to say that *time* is a noun and *flies* a verb, but in the joke that *time* is a verb and *flies* a noun. We can justify this of course by comparing the sentence on the first interpretation to *John runs*, etc., but in the second to *run races*, etc. But in doing this we are not merely finding the constituents, we are giving labels to them. This kind of labelling can be used to differentiate the two possibilities in an example that is often quoted against IC-type analysis:

Flying planes can be dangerous.

If we see that we have the contrast between

Flying planes is dangerous.
and   *Flying planes are dangerous.*

it becomes clear that in the one case *flying* is the head of the noun phrase, while in the other the head is *planes*. In the first both *flying* and *planes* are nouns, in the second *planes* is a noun and *flying* an adjective. Another example of exactly the same type is:

Visiting relatives can be a nuisance.

Often we find that there are ambiguous pairs that differ not only in the IC analysis but also in the labels. An excellent example is yet another well known linguistic pair, which however has to be said not written – *The sun's rays meet | The sons raise meat.* These are identical in speech, but the first ICs are either *The sun's rays | meet* or *The sons | raise meat.* Clearly also *rays/raise* is a noun in the first and a verb in the second, while *meet/meat* is a verb in the first and a noun in the second. Similar arguments hold for another example that has often been quoted – *What worries me is being ignored by everyone.* This can clearly mean either that 'I am worried by being ignored by everyone' or that 'everyone is ignoring the thing that worries me'. The crucial IC point is whether we analyse the last part of this sentence as *is being ignored | by everyone* or *is | being ignored by everyone,* and, in labelling terms, whether *being ignored* is part of the verbal constituent *is being ignored,* or the nominal constituent *being ignored by everyone.*

Once we start to use 'labels' we have clearly left simple analysis and are undertaking analysis that is similar to traditional parsing, the division of sentences into already established grammatical elements. This kind of analysis is today usually referred to as a 'phrase structure grammar'. It shows some of the weaknesses of IC analysis that we have been discussing. In particular it still seems to assume that the elements are in sequence. For that reason they can still be shown by a tree diagram, a 'phrase structure' tree diagram with all the 'nodes' (where the branches branch out) labelled. The phrase structure tree for our first example is given on the next page. But notice that we do not always have labels available. If *a young man* is a noun phrase what shall we call *young men*? And if *the girl with a blue dress* is a noun phrase is *the girl* still a noun phrase? (Though here we should, perhaps, distinguish between 'simple' and 'complex' phrases, the latter being composed of more than one simple phrase – see p. 76.)

There are sophisticated versions of phrase structure grammars. The three best known are 'Scale and category' associated with the name of Michael Halliday in London University, 'Tag-

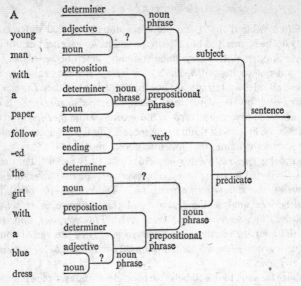

memics' associated with the name of Kenneth Pike of Michigan, and 'Stratificational grammar' associated with Sidney Lamb of Yale. It would be impossible to do justice to any of them in a book of this kind. All three, however, go well beyond simple phrase structure; their analysis cannot be simply presented on phrase structure trees with the appropriate words and morphemes at the end of the branches. But it would seem that in all three the basic assumption is that language consists to a very large extent of elements in sequence. These theories thus are essentially extensions of, rather than radical alternatives to, IC analysis. In the next chapter we shall consider a more radical departure.

4. Transformational-Generative Grammar

In 1957 Noam Chomsky's *Syntactic Structures* was published. This was the book that first introduced to the world the most influential of all modern linguistic theories, 'transformational-generative grammar', TG for short. The theory was, undoubtedly, revolutionary, but as with all revolutions, some of it had already been foreshadowed in earlier works, particularly in the writings of Chomsky's own teacher, Zellig Harris, and even in the writings of some scholars who were and have remained within a theoretical framework that seems utterly opposed to that of TG. Since 1957 Chomsky has modified his views and has on the whole moved even further away from the American linguistics of the 1940s and 1950s, especially in the more philosophical aspects of his theory, but much of what is important can still be found in *Syntactic Structures* and an understanding of the linguistics of that time therefore requires reference to this book.

The name 'transformational-generative' suggests, quite rightly, that there are two aspects of the theory. The grammar it provides is both 'transformational' and 'generative'. These two aspects are not logically dependent upon each other, though the theory gains plausibility from the interaction of the two. But the two aspects can and should be considered separately. The transformational aspect is the more fundamental and perhaps more revolutionary and we shall, therefore, begin with that.

4.1 Transformation

The grammatical theories which we have so far been discussing were concerned very largely with the analysis of sentences in the sense that they must be divided into parts and that the functions of the various parts must be stated. This was not of course an end in itself. Analysis of this kind allowed the investigator to show how one sentence was related to another in that their descriptions would be partly alike and partly different. If, for instance, we consider the sentences *John likes Mary* and *John liked Mary* the difference consists solely in the occurrence of *-s* rather than *-d*, or, to put it more technically, of the present tense morpheme rather than the past tense one. We can show this in a diagram quite simply:

$$\textit{John like} \begin{Bmatrix} \textit{-s} \\ \textit{-d} \end{Bmatrix} \textit{Mary}$$

There were morphemic problems of the kind we have already discussed, e.g. of *take* and *took* (p. 117), but the rather complex solutions proposed were intended to handle these. The difference between *I take a look* and *I took a look* would for many linguists have been simply that the second sentence contains the past tense morpheme (even if what the relevant morphs are was a matter of considerable dispute).

There are, however, plenty of sentences in English which seem to be very closely related, but whose relationships cannot be handled in this way. The most striking examples of this kind are the pairs of active and passive sentences such as

> *John saw Mary,*
> *Mary was seen by John,*

or   *The teacher allowed all the little children to go out to play,*
> *All the little children were allowed to go out to play (by the teacher).*

Not only are these pairs of sentences related, perhaps even more closely than the present tense/past tense pairs we considered earlier, but also we can talk with some plausibility of the passive sentences being 'formed from' the active ones or even of being 'the passive of' the active ones. Yet there is no way in which their analysis in terms of any kind of phrase structure grammar can show this relationship. Indeed there were some linguists who actually denied that active and passive sentences were related grammatically and insisted that the relationship was purely semantic, i.e. that they merely had (roughly) the same meaning.

What we need then is a theory that will not merely allow us to replace one element by another or by a number of others, but also to take the sentence and completely rearrange it. We have to note then, in order to relate the first pair of sentences, that in the first of them (the active one) *John* comes before the verb and *Mary* after the verb, while in the second (the passive) *Mary* comes before the verb and *John* after the verb, preceded by *by*, and that this change in relative position is to be accounted for in the grammar. (In traditional terms *John* is the subject and *Mary* the object of the active sentence while *Mary* is the subject and *John* the 'agent' – perhaps, as there is no common technical term – of the passive sentence.)

We can make a general statement about these relations. We can, that is, state how we convert an active sentence into a passive sentence: we have to change the position of the nouns or noun phrase and insert *by* before the second one in the passive and at the same time change the verb from active into passive. This Chomsky refers to as a 'transformation'. In *Syntactic Structures* he handles the active passive relationship by saying that:

'If S_1 is a grammatical sentence of the form

$$NP_1 - Aux - V - NP_2$$

then the corresponding string of the form

$$NP_2 - Aux + be + en - V - by + NP_1$$

is also a grammatical sentence.'

The symbols should not deter us here. S_1 means the 'first sentence', i.e. the first sentence we might consider – others would be labelled S_2, S_3, etc. NP_1 and NP_2 refer to the first and second noun phrase in the first sentence – in our examples *John* and *Mary* or *the teacher* and *the little children*. V stands for verb. Aux refers to tense and all auxiliary verbs, while be + en (*en* stands for the part participle) provides the passive element (see p. 77). The dashes and plus signs can be ignored.

The point that has to be stressed is that in this way we can relate *John saw Mary* and *Mary was seen by John*, but that no similar relationship holds between *John saw Mary* and *Mary saw John*. These last two sentences have the same structure and make use of the same words, but that is all. They are no more closely related, apart from this, that *John saw Mary* and *Bill saw Mary*. The reason for stressing this is that, as we have seen, given an active sentence we can always, or with only very rare exceptions, proceed to its passive transform, but given a sentence of the type *John saw Mary* it does not follow at all that a sentence of the kind *Mary saw John* is equally possible. This is very clear from the fact that we can say *John ate an apple* but not **An apple ate John*. Similarly (an example from the literature on the subject) though we may have *Casals plays the cello* and *The cello is played by Casals* we shall not find **The cello plays Casals* or **Casals is played by the cello*.

It was in order to handle relations of this kind that the notion of transformation was introduced. In the simplest form of the theory a transformation can be thought of as transforming one sentence into another. The first of these sentences is known as a 'kernel' sentence. Active sentences were thus kernel sentences and passives were 'transforms' of them. (We shall see later, p. 169, that it is not strictly correct to talk about kernel sentences being transformed, and indeed that the notion of kernel sentence has become much less important in the theory. But for illustration the notions of kernel sentences and of their transforms are useful, and I shall, therefore, discuss the problem in these terms.)

Active and passive sentences are common in many languages though the precise features that distinguish them vary considerably. In Latin, for instance, and many other languages, it is not merely (or essentially) a matter of the order of the words, but of the cases (nominative, accusative, ablative) of the nouns. Active and passive is, par excellence, a transformational relationship. For if a linguist were to describe a language in which he stated that there were active and passive sentences but that active and passive involved no transformations, it would be difficult to see why he had used the terms 'active' and 'passive'. Suppose we had two sentences such as *John Mary saw* (meaning 'John saw Mary') and *John Mary was seen* (meaning 'Mary was seen by John') would we really decide that these were active and passive respectively? Would not the more obvious solution be that they were both active but that there was some difference of meaning, perhaps focus on *John* in the first and on *Mary* in the second. What is important is that in the active-passive relationship there must be some clear sense in which the object of the active sentence 'becomes' the subject of the passive.

There are, however, plenty of other transformations. One that occurs in English but is not paralleled in most languages is that of question, e.g. *Has John seen Mary?*, a transform of *John has seen Mary*. Here we have simple transfer of *has* (what is technically described as 'permutation'). This occurs with all the auxiliary verbs of English cf. *Is John coming? Can John come? Must I go?* etc. There is an interesting complication in that if there is no auxiliary verb, the verb DO has to be supplied to act as one (it is thus an 'empty' auxiliary, acting as an auxiliary simply because the grammar requires one), e.g. *John comes./Does John come? John came./Did John come?* (see also p. 173). It happens that French and German employ a similar device, though without the restriction that only auxiliary verbs can be transposed (though French has some restriction on pronouns and would not normally allow **Viens-je?*). But most languages have no similar question transformation. Questions are either marked by the intonation alone as in Spanish, or by a word which is itself the mark of question (as in Latin, Russian and many African languages).

So far we have been concerned only with transforming one sentence into another. A different and in some ways more important type of transformation involves more than one kernel sentence. This handles the problem of coordination and subordination that we briefly discussed in 2.4. Let us consider subordination in some detail. We saw there that there was a sense in which one sentence could be regarded as being part of another sentence, that one sentence could be 'embedded' into another. Our examples were:

>   *He said that he was coming*
> and *The boy who was standing there ran away*.

In the first of these we can see clearly that *that he was coming* functions as if it were a noun phrase, the object of *said*. We can, therefore, derive this sentence from two kernel sentences

>   *He said* ...
> and *He was coming*.

All we need to do is to put *he was coming* in the place of the space and add *that*. Similarly, the second sentence can be treated as a transformation of the two sentences

>   *The boy ran away*
> and *The boy was standing there*.

Since the traditional grammars talk about clauses beginning with *who* as 'relative clauses', we talk about the 'relative' transformation which places the second sentence after *boy* in the first and then replaces *the boy* in the second (the 'embedded' sentence) by *who*.

There is an important, if obvious, condition on the relative transformation. We must have the same noun phrase (*the boy*) in both sentences and could not, for instance, carry out the transformation from the kernel sentences *The boy ran away* and *The girl was standing there*. This may seem almost too obvious, but obvious points like this make clear what we can and what we cannot do.

A slightly different example is provided by

>   *I want John to come*.

Here clearly we have to think in terms of

>   *I want* ...
> and *John comes*.

where the space in the first sentence would normally be filled by a noun phrase, but in this case has to be filled by a transformed version of the second sentence. We could, therefore, write the first as *I want NP* and then say that the NP is replaced by the second sentence with the further condition that the finite verb *comes* is replaced by the infinitive *to come*. Note that in a similar way we can derive

> *I want to come.*

from *I want ...*
and *I come.*

with an additional device, that of deleting *I* in the second sentence. Starting with the two kernel sentences we arrive at the transform by three stages

(1) *I want   I come* (embedding)
(2) *I want I to come*   (replace *come* by *to come*)
(3) *I want to come*   (delete *I*)

As we have noted, this is known technically as embedding. The sentence that is embedded into the other is known as the 'constituent' and the sentence into which it is embedded as the 'matrix'.

The relevance of transformational grammar becomes even more obvious when we see the way in which it can disambiguate (resolve ambiguity in) sentences. We saw that IC analysis can sometimes disambiguate, as in the example *The old men and women* (see p. 127). But because sentences that appear to be identical are often transforms from different kernels, transformation analysis can disambiguate far more. A particular source of ambiguity arises from the fact that after transformation the overt marks of active and passive are often lost. A notorious example is *The shooting of the hunters was terrible.* Here we cannot tell whether this means that the way in which the hunters shot was terrible or that the fact that the hunters were shot was terrible. The transformation involved is a 'nominalizing' one, one that transforms a sentence into a nominal phrase. The relevant nominal phrase here is *The shooting of the hunters* which is the subject of *... was terrible*, and as such has been embedded into the sentence. But the kernel sentences from which this noun phrase is to be derived are either

> *The hunters shot (something)*
> or *The hunters were shot.*

A similar distinction, though not involving ambiguity, is to be found in

> *He likes watching*
> and *He needs watching.*

Here again we have to distinguish the embedded sentence in terms of active and passive. We have the kernel sentences

> *He likes* and *He watches*
> but *He needs* and *He is watched* (or *Somebody watches him*).

Note incidentally that the distinction can be found with a single verb WANT though with a different construction – *He wants to watch* vs. *He wants watching.*

To account for facts of this kind a distinction between 'surface structure' and 'deep structure' can be made (and this has become important – see pp. 185–6), the surface structure being that which is more immediately obvious and the deep structure that which takes into account the transformation. Ambiguous sentences such as *The shooting of the hunters was terrible* have the same surface structure, but different deep structures. Similarly, apart from having different verbs, *He likes watching* and *He needs watching* are identical in surface structure but different in deep structure.

A different problem is presented by the two sentences

> *I expected the doctor to examine John*
> *I persuaded the doctor to examine John.*

These two sentences clearly have the same surface structure and do not seem to involve any active/passive contrasts in the deep structure. Nevertheless the active and passive relationship is important as a criterion for establishing a difference here in deep structure. It is clear that *the doctor to examine John* is an embedded sentence. The passive of this would be *John to be ex-*

amined by the doctor. We cannot, however, apply this transformation to both the sentences to give us:

> *I expected John to be examined by the doctor*

and *I persuaded John to be examined by the doctor.*

The first of these two sentences provides no problem. Nothing more has been done than is usually involved in the passive transformation. But in the second there is a complete change of meaning, since it is now John instead of the doctor who is the object of my persuasion. In some way we must, then, restrict the application of the passive transformation to the embedded sentence. What we want to say is that with *persuade*, but not *expect*, *the doctor* is the object of *persuade* but also the subject of *examine*. We can show this by proposing an analysis in terms of the kernel sentences

> (1) *I expected . . .*

and *The doctor examines John,*

> (2) *I persuaded the doctor . . .*

and *The doctor examines John.*

Our transformations then allow us to embed the second sentence into the first but with the restriction that, with *persuade*, the object of the matrix sentence and the subject of the constituent must be the same (*the doctor* in our example). We cannot, that is to say, apply this transformation to the two sentences

> *I persuaded the doctor,*
> *John is examined by the doctor,*

where we have transformed the second sentence into the passive (though we can then produce a totally different sentence

> *I persuaded the doctor that John should be examined by him*).

In contrast we can transform *the doctor examines John* into the passive with *expect* since there is no similar restriction. The same set of kernel sentences will therefore lead to both

> *I expected the doctor to examine John*

and *I expected John to be examined by the doctor.*

We can now return to some of the examples we discussed in the chapter on ICs. For a transformational analysis will prove much more illuminating even where bracketing or labelled bracketing will resolve ambiguity. Let us consider again

Flying planes can be dangerous.

We want to distinguish here two senses – the action of flying planes can be dangerous, and planes which fly can be dangerous. We can show this by differences in the matrix and the constituent sentence as well as the place of embedding. On the first meaning we have as kernel sentences

> *. . . can be dangerous*
> and   *(Someone) flies planes.*

We then transform the second into *flying planes* and insert it in place of NP. On the second meaning the kernel sentences will be

> *Planes can be dangerous*
> and   *Planes fly.*

Here we must apply a transformation similar to the relative transformation; one solution indeed would be to use this transformation to give us first

Planes which fly can be dangerous

and then a further transformation to give the required sentence by transforming *which fly* into *flying* and placing it before *planes*. These details are, perhaps, tedious; what is important is that we see that the deep structure of the two apparently identical sentences is quite different.

Another sentence in which we can resolve an ambiguity by transformation is:

John found the boy studying in the library.

In terms of meaning, the ambiguity depends on whether in the library was the place where John found the boy or whether John found the boy who was studying in the library. The ambiguity is quite easily resolved by transforming into the passive:

> *The boy was found studying in the library* (*by John*).
> *The boy studying in the library was found* (*by John*).

Note that this is a slightly new principle; we establish them as having different deep structure because they have different passives. We do not, of course, necessarily have to find one sentence with two possible meanings to exemplify grammatical ambiguity. For instance, let us suppose that the sentence we have been considering has only the first transformation (and indeed it is by far the more likely), i.e. only

> *The boy was found studying in the library* (*by John*).

We can then compare, to indicate the differences of deep structure,

> *John knew the boy studying in the library*,

for the only possible transformation is:

> *The boy studying in the library was known* (*by John*)

and not

> **The boy was known studying in the library* (*by John*).

Another pair of sentences that can take us into a very complex problem is:

> *He is eager to please.*
> *He is easy to please.*

Again we seem to have the active/passive contrast

> *eager   he pleases* (*someone*)
> *easy   he is pleased*   or   (*someone*) *pleases him.*

However, this is not the only difference between these two sentences. Let us look deeper and so illustrate how complex are some of the transformational relations in English (or in any language for that matter). With *eager* we can set up the kernel sentence

> *He is eager . . .*

or perhaps

He is eager for . . . (as in *He is eager for a walk*)
and   *He pleases* (*someone*).

But it is not at all plausible to propose

> *He is easy for* . . .
> (*Someone*) *pleases him.*

Instead we want to relate the sentence to

> *It is easy to please him,*

or even to

> *To please him is easy.*

If this is so we have to say the kernel sentences are

> . . . *is easy*
> (*someone*) *pleases him.*

We then have to apply transformations, first of all to place the constituent sentence in the matrix and then to transform again from *To please him is easy* to *He is easy to please.*

A few years ago there was a lively discussion on the deep structure of sentences of this kind, for there seems here to be 'multiple ambiguity'. I cannot go into all the possibilities in detail, but a brief look at some will be helpful. Let us take first

> *It is too hot to eat.*

We can again think in terms of

> *It is too hot* . . .
and   — *eats* —

But what is the relation between *it*, the subject of the matrix sentence, and the blanks (the subject and object) of the constituent? It depends, of course, on what is referred to by *it* – it could be the weather or the dog or the food. With *weather* it is neither subject nor object, with *dog* it is subject, with *food* it is object:

> *It is too hot for* . . .

weather: (*someone*) eats (*something*)
dog: *dog eats* (*something*)
food: (*someone*) eats *food*.

In all three cases we can transform to

> *It is too hot to eat.*

In all of these, however, the matrix sentence is of the same type as *He is eager to please*:

> *He is eager for ...*
> *It is too hot for ...*

though with *eager*, *he* can only be the subject of the constituent sentence and there is no ambiguity.

But there are also some more sentences in which the matrix is of the same type as *He is easy to please*, i.e. ... *is easy*. Let us consider the ambiguity in

> *It is easy to call* (i.e. calling is easy)

and   *It is easy to call* (i.e. the dog can be easily called).

We are now thinking in terms of

> ... *is easy*

and   — *calls* —

The ambiguity can be made clear by the paraphrases

> *To call is easy.*
> *To call the dog is easy.*

What then is the relation between *it* and the subject and object of the embedded sentence? The answer would seem to be either that it can be neither subject nor object, or that it can be the object:

> (*Someone*) calls (*someone*).
> (*Someone*) calls *the dog*.

In both cases we can transform into *It is easy to call*. There is a striking difference between this and the *It is too hot to eat* example:

it does not seem possible to have *it* referring to the SUBJECT of
the embedded sentence. If we have to embed a sentence like

> *The ape calls*   (*someone* or *something*)

we shall not produce

> *It is easy to call*

but·instead

> *It is easy for it to call*

Note that there is no obvious reason why *It is easy to call* should
not have threefold ambiguity as does *It is too hot to eat*. It is
simply a fact of English that there is no complete parallelism between the two structures.

Sometimes ambiguity involves both of the two kinds of transformation that we have just been considering as well as the subject object relations. Consider, for example,

> *It is hard to read*

which may mean either that reading is hard or that it, the book,
is hard to read. We then have the double contrast of

> *. . . is hard*
> (*someone*) *reads* (*something*)

and *It is hard for . . .*
> (*someone*) *reads it*.

If such an apparently simple construction is so complex the need
for thinking in transformational terms is obvious.

Before we end this section there are two important theoretical
points that must be made. It is not claimed that none of these
ambiguities can be resolved without transformations. Some of
them can be resolved by IC analysis. In the case of *John found
the boy studying in the library* it is a matter of whether the second
IC cuts are between *found* and *the boy studying in the library* or
between *found . . . studying in the library* and *the boy*. In the case
of *Flying planes can be dangerous*, although the ICs alone do not
resolve the ambiguity, it is resolved once they are handled in

terms of the labelled ICs head and modifier since we have either

	adjective-noun	(planes which fly)
or	noun(gerund)-noun	(to fly planes).

We could perhaps argue that there are not merely two different deep structures here, but also two different surface structures. Moreover, the distinction between these can be established by seeing whether *flying* or *planes* is the subject of the verb by substitution of *is* or *are* for *can be*:

> *Flying planes are dangerous.*
> *Flying planes is dangerous.*

None of these remarks invalidates the claims of transformational analysis. What is really important is not that we have different classes of words or that we have to choose between *is* and *are*, but rather that we ought to distinguish the two possibilities of *Planes fly . . .* and *fly planes*. Nevertheless, some ambiguities can only be resolved by transformation. No IC type analysis of which I am aware can disambiguate *The shooting of the hunters* or *It is too hot to eat*. Each of these surely has only ONE surface structure but two or more deep structures.

The second point is that although we have spoken about meaning there is no need to base the justification for transformation upon meaning. It should certainly be agreed that a grammar that fits more neatly into semantics is better than one which does not, but grammar should not be based on semantics. We do not want to justify the passive transformation by saying that the active and the passive have the same meaning. The essential point rather is the one that Chomsky made, that any active sentence (with rare exceptions) can be transformed into a passive one.

In this way transformational grammar is still formal in the sense in which the term was used in 1.4. The relation between active and passive involves a very different set of features from the relation between past and present, but they are no less matters of form of the language. Transformational grammar allows us to state all kinds of relationships that could not otherwise be stated. There is, as a result, the possibility that it may be used to handle features that are better treated as purely semantic. Some modern work that has developed from TG has gone a long way from its original concept and deals with much that would certainly have been regarded as purely semantic a few years ago (see, pp. 185-8).

4.2 Generation

The second characteristic of TG is that it is 'generative'. This means that a grammar must 'generate all and only the grammatical sentences of a language'. We must not, however, be misled by this term. It does not mean that a grammar will, in fact, literally (at any time) bring all these sentences into existence. It means merely that the grammar must be so designed that by following its rules and conventions we could produce all or any of the possible sentences of the language. To 'generate' is thus to 'predict' what could be sentences of the language or to 'specify' precisely what are the possible sentences of the language. Thus a grammar should 'generate', 'specify', 'predict' sentences such as

John saw Mary,
I like ice-cream,

but not

     *Saw John Mary,
     *Like ice-cream I,
or **John seemed Mary,*
     *I read ice-cream.

There are two important aspects of a generative grammar both lacking, in some degree, in the previous traditional and structuralist grammars.

First, a generative grammar is not concerned with any ACTUAL set of sentences of the language but with the POSSIBLE set of sentences. We are not, then, concerned solely or even primarily with any observed sentences that have occurred, but rather with those that can, or could have occurred. The importance of this point is that some previous linguists had maintained that if they were to adopt a wholly scientific or empirical approach they must confine their attention to a 'corpus', or body of texts, usually a set of recordings or a set of transcribed texts. The researcher had first to go out and collect such a body of texts and then analyse them in detail. In theory, everything that was in the corpus had to be accounted for and anything that was not could and should be ignored. This could hardly be said to describe a LANGUAGE. It was more a description of an accidentally and arbitrarily selected set of utterances in that language. All kinds of interesting features may have been left out; the texts may have no examples of the plural form of many of the nouns and even some of the names of the days of the week. Even the most carefully collected and comprehensive sets of texts would have some gaps and could hardly result in a description of a complete language.

The advocates of TG have pointed out that any corpus has a finite number of sentences, no matter how large, yet a language consists of an infinite number of sentences. This infinity is a result of what is known as 'recursion' – that we can apply the same linguistic device over and over again. A typical example of recursion is found in the nursery rhyme *This is the house that Jack built. This is the corn that lay in the house that Jack built. This is the rat that ate the corn that lay in the house that Jack built. This is the cat that* ... We can continue *ad infinitum*, for whenever we stop we can always add another section to what has gone before. Similarly we can, in theory, add adjectives *ad infinitum* – *the old man, the little old man, the clever little old man* and so on. To prove to anyone who does not believe in the infinity of the number of sentences in a language, we have merely to ask him to give us the longest sentence he can produce and then add another adjective or relative clause to it. (In a similar way it can be shown that the set of numbers in mathematics is infinite: take the greatest possible number, and add one.)

To say that the number of sentences is infinite does not mean, of course, that the grammar itself is infinite. On the contrary, it has a finite number of rules just as the finite set of figures 0–9 allows us to generate the infinite set of numbers.

Secondly, to say that a grammar is generative is to say that it is explicit; that is, that it EXPLICITLY indicates just what are the possible sentences of the language. By its rules or conventions it generates all the sentences, but this is possible only if these rules or conventions are totally explicit, leaving nothing out, leaving nothing to chance, above all leaving nothing to the reader's intelligence or to his knowledge of the language or of the way in which languages usually work. It has sometimes been argued that TG is essentially grammar for the computer. This is, in fact, not true, and in some ways a TG analysis is not in a convenient form for programming into a computer. But there is one relevant point. A computer is recognizably a 'moron'; it will do nothing except what it is told to do, and cannot, therefore, use a grammar to generate sentences if any part of the instructions have been left out. A very good test of explicitness of a grammar would be, then, whether it was one that could be fed to a computer.

This, too, is a reaction against previous approaches. A grammar that looks for patterns in a body of texts could fail to be explicit even if it allowed for considerable extrapolation. For to a very large degree it would be left to the reader to see that the patterns could be extended to other forms of the language, but to make use of the reader's knowledge in this way is to fail in explicitness. The traditional grammars exemplify the point well. In the Latin grammar the conjugations of the verbs and the declensions of the nouns are set out in long paradigms, each conjugation or declension taking examples from one verb or noun, and then indicating that other verbs and nouns belong to the same conjugation or declension. But what does it mean to say that *porta* 'door' belongs to the same declension as *mensa* 'table', whose forms are given as examples of the first declension? It is left to the student to use his intelligence to reconstruct the forms of *porta* by analogy. This is to fail the test of explicitness.

Within morphology this may not be very important. It is usually easy enough to reconstruct such forms. But in syntax there is a great deal that is omitted, precisely because without the explicitness criterion investigators have failed to ask themselves what is and what is not possible. Many grammars have neglected this point. It is not at all clear from them that such items as *interesting this book* or even *He very ran* are impossible in English.

We must not, however, be too hard on previous linguists. They had not all been entirely unaware of the difference between studying a set of texts and studying a language. A few had, it is true, taken a set of texts as the totality of their data and carried out an 'inductive' analysis of them. But most scholars had used texts only as a guide to the language and often went beyond them. In the first place, it is common for an investigator to fill 'gaps' in his grammar by asking an informant questions. Supposing, for example, there was no example of the plural form of the word for 'horse', though the language had singulars and plurals. He would then either ask his informant direct, if the informant was sufficiently sophisticated, or devise a sentence which would elicit it more naturally. Secondly, he would often assume that patterns established in one part of the grammar worked for another similar part. For instance, if a language had a very complex verbal system, the investigator would not think it necessary to attest every single form of every single verb; this would be an almost impossible task in some 'highly inflectional' languages. Instead he would first work out the paradigm in full for one verb, then look to see if there were verbs which differed and so set up verb classes. He would note what were the essential differences without checking every single form of every single class and would assign all verbs to one or other of the classes on the basis of a few essential differences in a few forms. Of course, he might prove to have been mistaken; he might fail to notice that one verb had a completely irregular form for, say, the second person dual of the imperfect subjunctive passive. But this kind of anomaly is so unlikely that it can safely be discounted. The rarer the form the more likely it is to conform to a regular pattern; this is natural since the native speaker would otherwise be unable to retain a command of his language. Thus many scholars did in fact 'extrapolate' and did indicate in some degree what sentences were or were not possible. But on the whole they failed the test of explicitness, and unlike the generative grammarians did not regard 'prediction' as the most important part of their function as grammarians. Filling in 'gaps' is not quite the same as being generatively explicit. In a generative grammar it is the AIM of the grammar to go beyond any actual set of sentences and to state explicitly what the possible sentences are.

I suggested earlier that transformation and generation were not linked together logically. But there is one way in which a generative approach justifies transformation. In the previous sections I occasionally made references to the meaning of sentences in order to elucidate the transformations, but noted that transformations should not be justified in terms of semantics. TG as much as any other kind of grammar should be formal in the sense in which this term was defined in 1.5 (p. 40). The essential point about transformations is the one that Chomsky made with regard to the passive – that given any English active sentence we can with rare exceptions state that the corresponding passive (i.e. with the necessary changes) is equally an English sentence. But it is not true that for any English sentence a similar sentence with merely the verb changed from active to passive is also an English sentence. Alongside

> *I drink beer,*
> *She plays the piano,*

we shall not find

> **I am drunk by beer,*
> **She is played by the piano,*

but only

> *Beer is drunk by me,*
> *The piano is played by her.*

What this shows is that there are severe restrictions on the nouns that may co-occur with active verbs as subjects or objects, and, more important, that these co-occurrence restrictions are preserved by the passive transformation. Only those nouns that occur as subject with active verbs may occur after *by* with the passive and only those that occur as object with active verbs may occur as subjects with the passive. The restrictions must all be stated in a generative grammar, in the sense of a totally explicit grammar, for such a grammar must not generate the ungrammatical sentences given above. If we did not include passive transformations in our grammar these restrictions would have to be stated all over again for passive sentences. To generate sentences economically, therefore, transformations are essential because the same restrictions apply after the transformations have been carried out.

There are two other important points that are related to the whole question of generation. The first concerns the contrast between 'discovery' and 'evaluation', and the second the contrast between 'competence' and 'performance'.

Let us look first at discovery and evaluation. The structuralists were largely concerned, as we have seen, with the problem of how to DISCOVER the phonemes, morphemes, etc. of the language. Moreover they required that in the interest of 'empirical', 'scientific' linguistics we must begin with the observed data and work 'upwards' from the sound system to the grammatical system, keeping the two in their right place in the sequence and completely apart. (The sound system had to come first because it was felt that only the phonetic/phonemic aspects of language provided a basis for scientific statement, since meaning was outside the possibility of serious investigation.) This requirement was completely unjustified, and partly based upon a failure to distinguish between research procedures and grammatical descriptions. The research procedures may be in a particular order (though few today would consider that the order given by the structuralists was the right order, since they would no longer wish to exclude semantics), but the description should be presented in whatever way seems most adequate, beginning at either 'end' or in the 'middle'. Moreover, the description should be justified as a whole and not piecemeal with each section independent of each other and one section preceding another. The grammar depends on the phonology and the phonology on the grammar, and neither precedes the other. What linguistic theory has to provide is not a set of 'discovery procedures' – procedures for discovering the structure of the language – but a set of 'evaluation procedures', procedures for evaluating all the possible descriptions and saying why one is better than the others.

Once again, however, it is not wholly true that earlier linguists were unconcerned with evaluating their descriptions and simply concentrated on discovery. They, naturally enough, discussed why one solution was better than another, and this was evaluation. One famous article, in fact, dealt with 'Two models of grammatical description' and discussed in detail the merits and demerits of each. In London the 'school' of J. R. Firth had explicitly rejected 'methods' in favour of 'theoretical relevance'. In 1957 Firth had written 'The excessive use of methods and procedures is avoided so that theoretical relevance may not be hidden or obscured.' But it must be said that it was Chomsky who first clearly made the distinction between evaluation and discovery, and came down so firmly on the side of evaluation.

The second important point concerns 'competence' and 'performance'. This is related to the TG grammarians' interest not in the actual texts but in what is linguistically possible. Their interest does not lie, therefore, in the actual utterances of the native speaker of a language, but rather with what he CAN say. This concerns his 'knowledge' of the language, his 'competence', not what he actually does at any time, the sentences he actually produces, which are a matter only of 'performance'.

According to the theory, the native speaker of a language has 'internalized a set of rules' which form the basis of his ability to speak and to understand his language. It is the knowledge of these rules that is the object of the linguist's attention, not the actual sentences he produces. Of course, the linguist may well investigate the speaker's competence by observing what he says, but his actual utterances, which are part of his performance, are not themselves the object of his investigation but merely form part of the evidence for his competence.

The distinction between competence and performance is important in accounting for the fact that when we speak we often do not speak 'grammatically'. We change the sentence half way through, or we do not complete it, or we add bits that could not be justified on a careful grammatical description. It has, in fact, been estimated that a large proportion of spoken utterances are in this sense not grammatical at all. But the linguist, it is argued, is not concerned with these deviations, false starts, etc. He is concerned rather with the ideal form of the language which the native speaker 'knows', even if he seldom reproduces it exactly.

The competence/performance distinction is important also for understanding the point about the infinite number of sentences in a language. For it is obvious that although in theory we can go on for ever increasing the size of a sentence, there must be some practical limits. Once such limits are set, the number of sentences is no longer infinite. This limit then is not a matter of competence, but of performance. Although we may never, in fact, produce a sentence of a thousand words, such a sentence might not be ungrammatical; it might well be a truly grammatical sentence of the English language. What prevents us from ever producing it has nothing to do with our knowledge of the language, but simply our actual inability, the limitations of our memory, to produce it. Performance, not competence, is the limiting factor.

Interest in competence does not, however, imply that we know much about the way in which we actually speak or understand speech. It makes no claims (as yet at least) about the neurophysiological structure of the brain; it has, however, been argued that with its emphasis on competence linguistics is essentially part of psychology.

The distinction between competence and performance is of questionable value. Methodologically it has much to be said for it. Certainly we must concentrate on the sentences that are accepted as being sentences of the language and must ignore the countless aberrations of actual speech (or at least account for these in terms of the 'grammatical' sentences of the language). We discussed this problem in 2.4 (p. 72).

But there are some grave difficulties. To begin with, how do we establish what the speaker knows? The evidence would seem to lie in the utterances he produces. But the TG grammarian has no way of going beyond these utterances that was not available to previous linguists. All investigators except the few who limited themselves totally to the examination of actual texts have had the task of making generalized statements based upon the limited material they observed. They usually regarded their procedure as 'inductive', generalizing from the particular. This process would allow the exclusion of 'ungrammatical' sentences simply because they do not fit in with the more generalized statements. What more, then, have the TG grammarians to offer? One point is that they regard the native speaker's 'intuition' as part of the evidence for his knowledge. He can 'introspect' and so (a) establish which sentences are and are not grammatical, and (b) give some indication of the grammatical structure of his language. But this is very dangerous. Most native speakers if asked questions about their language will give replies in accordance with what they learnt at school. They will say, for instance, that *It's me* is ungrammatical and that English has three genders masculine, feminine and neuter, and three tenses present, past and future. It is however true that we cannot write a satisfactory grammar without using intuition, but this is the intuition of the LINGUIST about the way in which languages are constructed. The point here is that a grammar that did in fact generate all the possible sentences of a language but did so in a totally arbitrary or implausible way would not be acceptable. Such a grammar would be called 'weakly' generative. What is needed is a grammar that generates the sentences in such a way that it assigns to them the 'correct' structure. Such a grammar is 'strongly' generative. But the problem remains – how do we define 'correctness' here?

A second difficulty is that it is often not possible in practice to draw a line between competence and performance, precisely because we do not know whether certain sentences are possible, i.e. grammatical or not. If they occur are they evidence of the 'correct' grammatical structure or are they aberrations in our performance? There are many forms that seem to be half in and half out of grammar. What would be the reaction of many people to the question whether

He will have been being beaten

is grammatical or not? We can produce rules to show that this is a possible grammatical form; WILL can be combined with the perfect, the progressive and the passive and this will produce the necessary form. But supposing a native speaker rejects this. Is his rejection a matter of performance or competence? Is it that he knows the rules but cannot apply them here? Or is it that one of the rules he himself 'knows' is that the rules of combination do not allow will + perfect + progressive + passive? There seems to be no way of deciding this, and there are many such areas of 'fuzziness' in language. Even on the point about sentence length it is not clear that this is necessarily a matter of performance. The TG grammarians' argument is that there is no theoretical limit to the length of a sentence, but that the limit is set by performance features, in particular by the limitation of our memory. But it may be the case that the native speaker knows that sentences should not go beyond a certain level of complexity. He may, perhaps, not have an accurate assessment of the 'cut-off' point, but this is not really relevant. We may well know the difference between blue and green without being able consistently to draw a distinction with the blue-greens.

There are serious problems here. We can and must write grammars that both exclude ungrammatical sentences even if they have occurred and go beyond the material provided by any actual texts. How we proceed to do this should be a matter of great theoretical concern. We ARE concerned with competence rather than performance. But how do we establish the distinction? Merely to state that there is a difference and to give the labels 'competence' and 'performance' does not solve the problem. It only indicates that there is one.

There is one last but very important point that is often almost deliberately (one feels) misunderstood. To talk about a person's knowledge of his language can mean no more than his implicit knowledge, his ability to speak. It does not, or should not, suggest that he has explicit knowledge, knowledge of the kind that we acquire when we learn languages at school in the old fashioned way. When the native speaker of Welsh told me that as a learner of Welsh I knew much more Welsh than he did he was, of course, referring to explicit knowledge. But his implicit knowledge, his competence, was greater than any non-native speaker can ever have. The distinction is sometimes made in terms of 'knowing how' and 'knowing that'. We may well know how to swim without knowing anything about what we actually do when we swim. So knowledge of this kind in relation to our own language does not imply any ability to talk about the language, any knowledge of linguistic facts. If it is argued that native speakers do have some knowledge about their language in this other sense, that they are able to describe the facts of the language, this is either equivocation in the use of the word 'knowledge' or false. Native speakers of a language often know little or nothing about it, save what they were taught at school, which is at times wrong or largely irrelevant.

4.3 Rules

A full understanding of TG is possible only if there is an understanding of some of the technical devices used (and the technical problems). For in both its aspects of transformation and generation this kind of grammar requires rigorous formal procedures.

The theory was presented in its original form in *Syntactic Structures*; with certain modifications, this is the form that I shall discuss in this section. This original form which Chomsky now refers to as the 'classical' theory is on the whole easier to understand both in regard to the way it works and in its justification. The later form or forms of the theory will be dealt with briefly in the next section and will be seen, as they are best seen, as a development of the 'classical' theory.

Fundamental to TG is the notion of rule; TG is 'rule-based' grammar. The idea of 'rule' is, however, to be understood in the same way as 'generate' was understood. Rules are part of the device for generating the sentences of the language and owe their justification to the part they play in that generation. In this sense rules are not to be identified with the rules that are found in other types of grammar. In particular, they must be clearly distinguished from the rules of traditional normative grammar and from rules of a purely descriptive kind (though they have something in common with both).

As we saw in 1.3 the traditional grammars have many rules of the kind that tell us not to put prepositions at the end of a sentence, to say *It's I, He's bigger than I*, to use *whom* correctly, etc. These are all prescriptive or normative rules telling us what we 'ought' to do, i.e. what we ought to do if we accept the dictates of traditional grammar. Most of these rules have no validity beyond the fact that they have appeared in the grammars over the years and have been accepted by teachers and others, but in fact are based on Latin, pseudo-logic or pure invention. Clearly it is not rules of this kind that are now the subject of our attention.

Secondly, there are descriptive rules, generalizations about what actually happens in language. If, for example, we state that plural forms of nouns are, as subject, always followed by plural forms of verbs, or that uncountable nouns cannot be preceded by indefinite articles, these are rules based upon observation, inductive rules. However, since they are seldom one hundred per cent valid, 'rule' here has a meaning akin to that of 'rule' in the expression 'as a rule'. Again our generative rules are not of this kind. They are not simply generalizations about language.

Nevertheless generative rules share some characteristics of both kinds of rule that we have just been discussing. They are in the first place instructions like the normative rules, but instead of being instructions for the production of 'correct' speech, they are instructions for generating all the possible sentences of the language. In the second place, like descriptive rules, they relate to the facts of actual languages, not the invented languages of grammarians, and are ultimately based, therefore, upon what people say rather than what they 'ought' to say.

The rules of TG are 'rewrite' rules. That is to say they rewrite one symbol as another or as several others (or one set of symbols by another set) until eventually the sentences of the languages are generated. Since we wish to generate sentences, the rules start with the symbol S (which stands for 'sentence'), and then a sequence of rules 'rewrite' this symbol until a sentence is produced. The rule itself is in the form of a symbol or set of symbols on the right-hand side, an arrow in the middle and a symbol or set of symbols on the left-hand side. The arrow is interpreted to mean 'rewrite'. Thus

$$A \to BC$$

means 'rewrite A as BC'.

Suppose we wish to generate in English the simple sentence *The man read a book*. A simple set of rules could be as follows:

(1) S   → NP + VP
(2) VP   → V + NP
(3) NP   → Det + N
(4) V   → read
(5) Det → the, a
(6) N   → man, book

Rule 1 begins with S (sentence) and rewrites it as NP (noun phrase) plus VP (verb phrase).
Rule 2 rewrites VP as V (verb) plus NP.
Rule 3 rewrites NP as Det (determiner) and N (noun).
So far we have generated only symbols standing for grammatical categories. The remaining rules convert these into words and morphemes.
Rule 4 converts V into *read*, Rule 5 Det into *the* or *a* and Rule 6 N into *man* or *book*. If we apply the rules in sequence we generate the following 'strings' successively:

S	
NP + VP	(Rule 1)
NP + V + NP	(Rule 2)
Det + N + V + Det + N	(Rule 3)
Det + N + read + Det + N	(Rule 4)
the + N + read + a + N	(Rule 5)
the + man + read + a + book	(Rule 6)

A set of rules of this kind is said to be a 'derivation' of a sentence, in this case of *The man read a book*. The term 'string' is used for the sequence of symbols, and the final string, beyond which the rules do not take us, is the 'terminal string'. The 'terminal string' in our example is *the + man + read + a +*

book, though as we shall soon see not all terminal strings can be identified with sentences. The elements of which the terminal strings are formed are known as 'formatives'; these are roughly equivalent to the structuralists' morphemes. They are either 'lexical' formatives – nouns, verbs, etc., – or 'grammatical' formatives. In fact, our example as analysed here has only lexical formatives, but if we had introduced an -*s* plural or an -*ed* past tense morpheme there would have been grammatical formatives. Plenty of examples of these will be found later.

There is one useful convention that may be mentioned at this point. We can indicate 'optional' elements by the use of brackets. Thus Rule 3 could be written as

$$NP \rightarrow Det\ (Adj) + N$$

This would say that NP may be rewritten either as Det + N or as Det + Adj + N. A further rule might be

$$Adj \rightarrow big,\ difficult$$

We can now generate such sentences as *The big man read a difficult book*.

Rules of this kind merely restate in a rather different way phrase structure analyses of the kind we discussed in Chapter 3. We can, in fact, re-interpret the rules given above in terms of a phrase-structure tree (see p. 134):

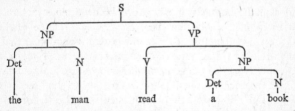

Representation of the phrase structure of a sentence in this way is known as its 'phrase marker', or, for short, P-marker.

In TG, phrase structure rules (as these are called), or PS-rules for short, form the basic part of the grammar and are technically described as the 'base component'. There are some other technical terms that may be noted. 'Node' refers to the places at which there is branching; the nodes are therefore indicated by the symbols NP, V, etc. A symbol or string is said to be 'dominated' by another symbol if the latter appears higher in the tree but in the same line of derivation. A symbol that is dominated by another has been expanded from it directly or indirectly in the rewrite rules. Thus *a* is dominated by Det, and also by NP and VP.

It will be apparent, perhaps, that the rules we have been discussing will generate many sentences other than the ones we want. We have the choice of both *a* and *the* for Det and *book* and *man* for N and, furthermore, both Det and N appear in two places in the rules and in the tree. They will therefore generate the sentences:

> *The man read the book.*
> *A man read a book.*
> *A man read the book.*

These sentences are grammatical, but the rules will also generate ungrammatical sentences of the kind (with similar variations with the determiners):

> **The book read the man.*
> **The book read the book.*
> **The man read the man.*

Almost all the grammars that have ever been written, structuralist and traditional, imply that these are sentences of the English language. It is, therefore, a virtue of a generative grammar that it makes quite clear, i.e. quite explicit, the fact that the rules of the grammar, as stated, will generate these ungrammatical sentences too. It then becomes possible to consider, as we shall see in the next section, how we can prevent such sentences from being generated by the grammar.

In TG discussions phrase structure plays two parts. First, it forms the base component of the grammar. Secondly, however, it has been argued that the chief criticism of the structuralist grammars is that they are all 'phrase structure' grammars, i.e. that they do not go beyond an analysis in phrase structure terms (whereas

TG has transformations and transformational rules). This argument is to some degree fair; the structuralists DID assume that language was of such a nature that it could largely be handled in such terms. Immediate Constituent analysis in particular was based upon this assumption. But many early grammarians made statements that went beyond the scope of phrase structure grammars and the criticism made by some of their TG opponents sometimes seems to be the unfair, question-begging line that as their grammars were all PS grammars they had no right to make many of the statements they claimed to make and that their grammars were by that token unsatisfactory!

Characteristically, then, TGs must contain not only phrase structure rules but also transformational rules (T-rules). As long as we are restricted to PS-rules we cannot generate passive sentences from active ones. We can, of course, if we wish, generate passive sentences by writing PS-rules to produce passive forms of the verb, but, as we noted in the previous section, this would mean that though we could generate both *John likes Mary* and *John is liked by Mary* by a similar set of rules, we should not in any way relate *John likes Mary* to *Mary is liked by John*. To do this we need a rule of a very different kind, not one that simply expands one symbol into another or others, but one that changes the order of the symbols. We will recall, in fact, that the passive transformation transformed

$$NP_1 - Aux - V - NP_2$$

into

$$NP_2 - Aux + be + en - V - by + NP_1 \quad \text{(see p. 137)}$$

We can write this as a rule:

$$NP_1 - Aux - V - NP_2 \rightarrow$$
$$NP_2 - Aux + be + en - V - by + NP_1$$

A more convenient way of writing this rule is:

Structural analysis $NP - Aux - V - NP$

Structural change $X_1 - X_2 - X_3 - X_4 \rightarrow$
$$X_4 - X_2 + be + en - X_3 - by + X_1$$

The effect is the same; we have merely indicated the element as numbered Xs and then shown how their order is changed.

There are two kinds of transformation, one involving single kernel sentences, the other two such sentences. The passive transformation is an example of the first; a single (active) kernel sentence is transformed into another (passive) sentence. But equally we want to generate sentences that involve co-ordination and subordination. We can, for instance, generate *John and Bill like Mary* from *John likes Mary* and *Bill likes Mary* by a simple rule that combines the two sentences:

Structural analysis $NP + Aux + V + NP$; $NP + Aux + V + NP$

Structural change $X_1 - X_2 - X_3 - X_4 - X_5 - X_6 - X_7 - X_8$
$\rightarrow X_1$ and $X_5 - X_2 - X_3 - X_4$

(In fact we can provide a much more general though more complex rule to account not only for this but also for *John likes and admires Mary, John likes Mary and Sue, John likes Mary and Bill likes Sue.*) Similarly, we can generate *I persuaded the doctor to examine John* from *I persuaded the doctor* and *The doctor examines John.* (Here the rule will have to delete one occurrence of *the doctor* and convert *examines* to *to examine.*) The rules involving one kernel sentence only are known as 'singulary' transformations, those involving two as 'generalized' transformations. Often, naturally enough, we shall need both to generate a sentence. For instance, our example in 4.1 *I persuaded John to be examined by the doctor* involves first the singulary passive transformation of *The doctor examines John* to *John is examined by the doctor* and then the generalized transformation that unites this sentence with *I persuaded John.*

There is a further distinction between two kinds of T-rules – obligatory and optional T-rules. The essential point here is that although the main justification for TG lies in the fact that it can generate among many others passive sentences from active ones, yet it cannot generate even all active sentences without recourse to some transformational rules. Some rules HAVE to be applied in order to produce sentences at all. These are, then, obligatory. On the other hand, we are not obliged to transform an active sentence into a passive one. If we generate an active sentence by our PS-rules alone we have a sentence. We may, if we please, transform it into another, a passive one. The rule, then, that converts active sentences into passive ones is optional. But PS-rules alone will not generate any sentence at all until a T-rule (an obligatory one) has been applied.

A good example of obligatory T-rules is provided by the element Aux which, as we saw above, is used to indicate the occurrence of auxiliary verbs and tense in English. English is notorious for having a very complex verbal system. It has very few inflections; we have only the contrast between *take*, *takes* and *took* for the verb TAKE. But it has also the progressive forms *is taking*, etc., the perfect forms *has taken*, etc. and all the forms with modals – *will take*, *shall take*, *may take*, *can take*, *must take*. Moreover, there are combinations of these. The form *would have been taking* is past tense (marked by *would*), perfect (marked by *have* and the past participle *been*), and progressive (marked by the occurrence of *be* in *been* and the *-ing* form of *taking*). There is a great deal of discontinuity here (see p. 129), since many of the categories are doubly marked by different words. If we consider, for instance, *have been taking* in our example the relevant parts are *have* and *-en* (marking the perfect), *be* and *-ing* (marking the progressive) and *tak-* indicating the verb. If we recognize all this in a generative grammar, the first rule that expands Aux is:

$$\text{Aux} \rightarrow \text{Tense (M) (Aspect)}$$

The parentheses indicate, of course, the optional elements. A verb MUST have a tense (past or present) but may or may not have a modal (indicated by M) or be progressive or perfect (these being referred to as Aspect). We have now to rewrite Tense as present or past. Present is then rewritten as either ø (zero) or *-s* and past as *-d*. If required, M is rewritten as *will* or *shall*, or *can*, etc., and Aspect as either *have* + *en* or *be* + *ing* or both. If we consider for instance the example above, *would have been taking*, we find

(1) past tense, (2) the modal *will*, (3) the perfect, and (4) the progressive, and we shall therefore rewrite Aux as:

$$d + will + have + en + be + ing$$

If we want to analyse the whole verbal phrase *would have been taking* we have to go back to an earlier rule to introduce the verb *take*. This would be:

$$V \rightarrow Aux + MV \text{ (main verb)}$$

with a later rule

$$MV \rightarrow take$$

The whole of the analysis so far can be represented by a tree diagram:

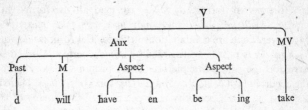

We have achieved this by using only PS-rules – no transformations as yet. It is obvious, however, that the elements are not in the right order if we are to generate an actual sentence. This is a result of the fact that we had used PS-rules to expand Aspect into SUCCESSIVE elements *have + en* and *be + ing*. *Have + en* and *be + ing*, however, represent discontinuous elements, which ought not to be in sequence at all. PS-rules can only place them in sequence; they cannot place discontinuous elements in their correct positions. We now have to place the elements in the required order, separating the *have* and the *en* by placing *en* after *be* and so on. This can be achieved fairly easily by the rule that says that wherever we have any verb (either a main verb or an auxiliary verb) preceded by an affix (and *s*, *ø*, *d*, *en* and *ing* are designated as affixes), the order of the two is to be reversed. Such a rule might read:

$$Af + V \rightarrow V + Af$$

We then get:

$$will + d + have + be + en + take + ing$$

A further set of rules of a slightly different kind (morpho-phonemic rules) will convert *will* + *d* into *would*, *be* + *en* into *been* and *take* + *ing* into *taking*, giving us the required *would have been taking*.

A rule such as $Af + V \rightarrow V + Af$ which changes the order of the elements is, of course, a T-rule not a PS-rule. But it is an obligatory T-rule; it has to be applied, since *d* + *will* + *have* + *en* + *be* + *ing* + *take* is not an English sentence. In contrast the passive transformation rule is an optional rule. We can generate English sentences without ever applying it because active sentences are perfectly grammatical sentences in English. All the other rules that we considered in 4.1 are equally optional.

The distinction between optional and obligatory transformations was important in the early form of the theory because most sentences cannot be generated without applying some of the obligatory T-rules. It will be remembered that in 4.1 it was remarked that, although we found it convenient to talk about the transformation of kernel sentences, this was strictly inaccurate. The point is that this implies (1) that the kernel sentences are sentences to which no transformations have been applied and (2) that the transformations were applied to kernel sentences. Neither assumption is correct. It is incorrect to say that kernel sentences are sentences to which no transformations have been applied, because even they have undergone obligatory transformations. The definition of the kernel sentence then has to be modified to being one to which no optional transformations have been applied. It follows that it is also misleading to talk about transformations being applied to kernel sentences at all. For it is obvious that the obligatory T-rules must operate AFTER the optional T-rule such as the passive transformation. For instance, the PS-rules might generate first

$$NP + Aux + V + NP$$

and then convert this by further PS rules into

John + present + have + en + see + Mary

The optional passive transformation next applies

Mary + s + have + en + be + en + see + by + John

The obligatory transformation then gives us

Mary + have + s + be + en + see + en + by + John

and the morphophonemic rules finally produce the required sentence. The passive transformation applies, then, not to kernel sentences at all, but to the terminal strings generated by the PS-rules that 'underlie' them.

An important characteristic of some rules is that they must be 'ordered', i.e. that one must be applied before another. In general, PS-rules are unordered. For instance, there is no essential ordering of the rules on p. 162. In fact some of the rules CAN only apply before others; we cannot rewrite VP as V + NP until we have first generated VP by the rule S → NP + VP, though on the other hand rules 4, 5 and 6 could be applied in any order. But this is not what is meant by 'ordered'. It would not matter how we ordered these six rules; there can be only one result, although by their intrinsic nature certain of the rules cannot apply until after others. To talk about 'ordered' rules implies that we MUST apply them in the correct order even though another order is possible, because if we apply them in the wrong order we shall generate different sentences. A very good example is provided by the rules for the concord of subject and verb and for the passive. We have to provide two rules, one the passive T-rule that we have already discussed, the other a concord rule that will introduce next to the verb a grammatical formative indicating singular or plural according to whether the preceding NP (the 'subject') is singular or plural. This rule is simple enough. It could be something like:

NP + sing + V → NP + sing + V + sing

But this rule must NOT be applied before the passive transformation. The reason is clear enough. If we wanted to generate *The men are mocked by the boy* our PS-rule will generate a terminal string

The + boy + sing + mock + the + men + plur

If we NOW apply the concord rule we shall introduce sing (singular) to the verb and this will remain when we apply the passive transformation. Our generated sentence will then be the ungrammatical **The men is mocked by the boy*. If, on the other hand, we apply the concord rule after the passive transformation the passive verb will, of course, agree with the NP that precedes it, the 'subject' of the passive not of the active verb.

In general the difference between PS-rules and T-rules seems clear enough, but it is to some extent a matter of definition. We can set out the things that a PS-rule cannot do:

(1) It cannot 'permute' symbols, i.e. change their order.
(2) It cannot 'delete' a symbol.
(3) It cannot rewrite more than one symbol at a time.
(4) It cannot add symbols.

None of the following rules, then, is permissible:

(1) XY → YX
(2) XY → X
(3) XY → ABC
(4) XY → XYZ

These restrictions (and others that are less obvious and more debatable) are largely justified in terms of the notion of derivation by a PS tree. All the non-permitted rules above fail to supply us with possible or unambiguous tree structures. The first implies crossing of branches which is not 'expansion'. The second implies that part of the tree provides no terminal elements at all, so why have it? The third would not give us an unambiguous derivation since we cannot tell whether BC is dominated by Y or AB dominated by X – the place of B in the derivation is wholly unresolved. The fourth is the reverse of the second – it creates a symbol from nowhere.

More importantly, however, PS-rules merely expand symbols generated by previous rules (as illustrated by the rules on p. 162), whereas T-rules do not. The passive T-rule, for instance, though it operates on a terminal string of the kind *The + man + read + a + book* nevertheless is not stated in terms of terminal symbols such as *the* and *man* but in terms of such symbols as NP, Aux, V – symbols used much higher in the derivation and which dominate *the + man*, etc. The reason is simple enough. The passive transformation takes the whole NP, whether it is *the man, John* or even *the silly little man that I spoke to the day before yesterday*, and places it after the verb. In this sense T-rules are said to operate upon 'variables' – symbols that may be expanded in various ways in the PS-rules, whereas PS-rules operate on constants – the actual symbols generated by the previous PS-rules. This is not a mere technical point. The T-rules refer to symbols higher up in the derivation, to symbols that dominate the previously generated strings rather than to the symbols that make up those strings, and thus require knowledge of the 'derivational history' of the symbols.

Nevertheless the distinction between PS- and T-rules is not always clear, or at least it is not always clear whether a particular feature ought to be handled in a PS- or a T-rule. Since there is no 'God-given' definition of the distinction between the rules, the ultimate criterion must depend on what we want them to do. An example is negation in English. How do we generate *He can't go* or *He isn't going* as compared with *He can go* and *He is going?* The most obvious answer might seem to be simply to introduce the element *not* into our PS-rules. A simple form of the rule could introduce *not* (as an optional element) along with Aux when we expand V:

$$V \rightarrow Aux \ (not) \ MV$$

By selecting or not selecting *not* we can produce either the negative or the positive sentences mentioned above. But there are problems with this simple solution. In the first place the verbs involved in negation are precisely those that are transposed to form questions, the auxiliary verbs, for example:

He isn't coming.	*Is he coming?*
He can't come.	*Can he come?*
He hasn't come.	*Has he come?*
We mustn't come.	*Must we come?*

But the question forms have to be generated by a T-rule since they involve permutation. It would seem at least very inelegant to handle two closely related features so differently, one using PS-rules, the other T-rules. Furthermore, if we have no auxiliary verb, we have to introduce a form of the verb DO. From *He comes* we generate not *He comes not or **He comesn't* but *He doesn't come*. Again there is a parallel situation with the questions since instead of **Comes he?* we have *Does he come?*

We now have to decide between two alternative solutions. We can introduce *not* into the PS-rules and account for the introduction of the DO forms by obligatory transformation rules like that which dealt with the affixes on p. 169. Alternatively, we can have an optional T-rule for negation paralleled with and closely associated with the optional T-rule for question. Such a rule would introduce the *n't* forms as well as the form of *do*. It is not clear which is the better solution. We might well wish to handle as much as we can in the PS-rules and so prefer the first solution, or we might prefer the second solution because of the similarity with the question transformation. (This point becomes relevant to our discussion in the next section.)

We have in this section concentrated almost entirely on syntax and said little about morphology. Nevertheless a generating grammar must be equally explicit about morphology and will contain, as we have already noted (p. 169), morphophonemic rules. The general form of these rules is clear enough. They will be of the type

$$will + d \rightarrow would$$
$$have + s \rightarrow has$$
$$take + d \rightarrow took$$

This easily disposes of many of the difficulties provided by the structuralists' approach to the morpheme. We do not, for instance, have to identify the morphs of *took*. Nevertheless with an inflected language such as Latin many problems remain. We could simply re-design the 'word and paradigm' method (p. 57) of saying that *audis* is the second person singular active form of AUDIO 'I hear' by having a rule:

$$audio + \text{2nd} + \text{sing} + \text{pres} + \text{act} \rightarrow audis$$

but this would totally fail to capture the generalizations that can be drawn from a comparison of this form with *amas* (first conjugation), *mones* (second conjugation) and *regis* (third conjugation) – that they all have final -*s*, that they differ in the vowels, *a*, *e*, *i* and *ī*. Somehow the rules have to be written to bring out these generalizations; it may perhaps be possible to identify the -*s* with second person so that we have a rule 2nd → s and the vowels with the verbs themselves. But there are many difficulties precisely because in inflected languages there is no one-to-one correspondence between grammatical category and form. Using a generative rule-based grammar may avoid some of the pitfalls of the morphemic approach but in itself it solves none of the difficulties. As yet comparatively little attention has been paid to these problems.

There is one final and crucial point. Do we really need T-rules at all, and if so why? We can generate all our passive sentences by PS-rules. *Mary was seen by John* can be generated by:

$$
\begin{aligned}
\text{S} \quad &\rightarrow \text{NP} + \text{VP} \\
\text{VP} \quad &\rightarrow \text{V} + \text{by} + \text{NP} \\
\text{V} \quad &\rightarrow \text{Aux} + \text{MV} \\
\text{NP} \quad &\rightarrow \text{Mary, John} \\
\text{Aux} \quad &\rightarrow \text{was} \\
\text{MV} \quad &\rightarrow \text{seen.}
\end{aligned}
$$

Why should we not want to do this? There are (at least) two answers, both of which were discussed in 4.2. The first is that there is intuitively a relationship between active and passive sentences, and a grammar would seem much more satisfactory if it generated the passive sentences via the active ones rather than independently, for independent generation through PS-rules shows a much closer relationship between *Mary saw John* and *Mary was seen by John* than between *John saw Mary* and *Mary was seen by John*. The second reason has greater implications for the theory. If we consider why *Casals plays the cello* and *The cello is played by Casals* are grammatical, while **The cello plays Casals* and **Casals is played by the cello* are not, it is clearly a matter of restriction between the nouns and verbs that function as the various NPs and MVs (the subjects, objects, etc.). But the restrictions are maintained after transformation; the nouns that may act as object of the active verb may act as the subject of the passive verb. Somewhere in the grammar these restrictions MUST be stated to avoid the generation even by the PS-rules of **The piano plays Casals* or **The book read the man*. The simple observation that these restrictions are preserved after transformation means that they need be stated once only, only for the kernel sentences. Without transformations they would have to be stated for all kinds of sentences generated by the PS-rules. These considerations are valid for all T-rules. We could (perversely) generate questions and all the sentences in 4.1 by PS-rules if we wished, but the restrictions on the co-occurrence of nouns and verbs, etc. would have to be stated independently for all the various structures that could (via T-rules) be handled together.

It even becomes plausible in the light of these remarks to treat in transformational terms structures that might seem to be appropriate to PS-rules. A simple example is the occurrence of adjectives before nouns. We could easily generate *the big man* by a PS-rule:

$$NP \rightarrow Det \ (Adj) \ N$$

But it can easily be seen that the adjectives that may occur in this position are almost precisely identical with those that, with the same noun, may occur in the 'frame' *The man is . . .* Thus we can have *the red book*, *The book is red*, but not **the liquid book* or **The book is liquid*; *the intelligent man*, *The man is intelligent* but not **the intelligent cloud* or **The cloud is intelligent*. (It might be possible to invent perverse contexts for some of these, but that is not really relevant; a grammar cannot really be expected to handle perverse or deliberately odd sentences.) The usual way, therefore, of generating adjectives before nouns is via a transformation from a kernel of the type *The man is big*. *The big man came* involves a generalized transformation from *The man came* and *The man is big*. There are exceptions to the general rule. We cannot generate *the last Dodo* from **The Dodo was last* or *the heavy smoker* from *The smoker was heavy*, nor will *The child is asleep* permit **the asleep child* (see pp. 64–5). But these are merely indications of the complexity of the situation. We must write the rules to generate only those combinations that ARE possible. We should, for instance, have to treat *asleep* as a different kind of element from the adjective, more like the prepositional phrase *in the garden*, and we might generate *the heavy smoker* from *He smokes heavily* rather than *The smoker is heavy*. As I suggested before, complexity is no argument against a theoretical approach if the complexity arises not out of the theory itself but out of the material which any theory ought to handle.

4.4 More recent developments

The theory presented in the previous section is, with only minor changes and additions for the sake of greater clarity, that presented by Chomsky in his *Syntactic Structures*: it is the 'classical' theory. In *Aspects of the Theory of Syntax*, which he published in 1965, the theory has changed and been developed in several striking ways.

The most fundamental change is that the notion of optional transformation is dropped for all the transformations that are of any real theoretical interest. We no longer transform an active sentence into a passive one by an optional transformation. Instead the element Passive is generated by the PS-rules (an optional element, of course, like Aspect, see p. 167). Then obligatory transformations carry out the changes needed – the provision of the passive form of the verb and the permutation of the relevant noun phrases (the subject and object). These are said to be 'triggered off' by the element Passive. For technical reasons the PS-rules generate not just Passive but *by* + Passive (thus introducing *by* here instead of via the transformation) so that one of the PS-rules, instead of being simply

$$VP \rightarrow V + NP$$

might read

$$VP \rightarrow V + NP (+ by + Passive).$$

To return to our example on p. 162 we can now generate not only the terminal string

$$the + man + read + a + book$$

but also, if we select the optional element

$$the + man + read + a + book + by + Passive.$$

But the occurrence of Passive forces us to apply obligatory transformations. In the simplest form the rule would be

$$NP_1 + Aux + V + NP_2 + by + Passive$$
$$\rightarrow NP_2 + Aux + be + en + V + by + NP_1$$

The final result would be the same as that produced by the rule on p. 165, i.e. *the book was read by the man*, but the route by which it has been achieved is different.

In some ways this change might seem to destroy the whole basis of TG, at least in so far as it claimed that its superiority over other grammars was that it was not simply a PS grammar. For now the relations that were handled solely in terms of transformations appear in the PS-rules. Passive is no longer a matter solely of transformations. It is also a matter of phrase structure.

Clearly there must have been good reasons for this fundamental change. There are, perhaps, as many as four. First, as we saw on p. 172, it is not at all easy to draw a clear line between those relations that should be handled in PS-rules and those that should be handled in T-rules. Is negation a matter of phrase structure in English or of transformation? In the new version of the theory none of these problems arise. Both negation and question are handled by introducing the optional elements Neg and

Q into the phrase structure rules. If either or both are chosen, obligatory transformations (introducing forms of DO where necessary) generate the correct sentences.

Secondly, the notion of optional transformation is likely to pose some problems when we try to relate our grammar to semantics. For while it is clear that the elements introduced by the phrase structure rules, lexical formatives like *man*, *book*, grammatical formatives like past and plural, all have some kind of meaning, it is not clear whether we can assign meaning to the optional transformations. Question may seem to have a meaning, but what about Passive? And in any case we have no theory that will relate meaning not only to elements generated by phrase structure rules but also to rules themselves (the optional T-rules). Obligatory rules, on the other hand, clearly have NO meaning. No meaning is added by placing affixes in their right places (p. 169) or by making sure that verbs agree with their subjects (p. 170). It is natural, therefore, to try to avoid the problems of the relations between rules and meaning by deciding that all transformations are obligatory and so devoid of meaning. Wherever there is choice (and so the possibility of meaning-differences) this is handled by the selection of items in the phrase structure.

Thirdly, a very great problem that was never seriously investigated concerns the way in which optional T-rules are applied. In a complex sentence we may well have a whole set of such rules. Our example *I persuaded John to be examined by the doctor* (pp. 142–3) involves two T-rules, one singulary, one generalized. But once we have applied a T-rule we change the terminal string in such a way that it can no longer be regarded as obviously derived from a phrase structure tree. This was, of course, precisely why we wanted transformations – we argued that passive sentences could not (plausibly) be generated by phrase structure rules. But if the transformed sentences are not generated by PS-rules, it would seem to follow that they can have no phrase structure. If however this is true, we cannot apply a second T-rule, for the really important point about T-rules is that they operate on clearly specified structures. The passive transformation, for instance, can be applied to

$$NP_1 + Aux + V + NP_2$$

but not to

$$NP_1 + Aux + V + Prep\ Phrase$$

where 'Prep phrase' stands for prepositional phrase, e.g. *in the garden*. We cannot, that is to say, produce a passive for *The man was standing in the garden*. There is clearly a real difficulty here since (1) transformations seem to destroy the phrase structure, (2) they themselves can only be applied to specific structures, (3) we need to have sequences of transformations. In the early form of the theory there were devices for indicating 'derived' phrase markers, suggesting that even after transformation the symbols could be treated in terms of phrase structure. But this is not only difficult to do; it is also in the nature of a desperate device to overcome an obvious defect. Again, of course, no problem arises if all transformations are handled first in the phase structure. What transformations may or may not co-occur can easily be stated there and the obligatory transformations that they 'trigger off' will provide the correct sentences.

The fourth point is that this new version of the theory contains a solution to a slightly different problem. In the earlier version *John was killed* has to be generated from *Someone killed John* via *John was killed by someone* with subsequent deletion of *by someone*. Similarly, it had to generate *I persuaded the doctor to examine John* from *I persuaded John* and *The doctor examines John*. But in the second of each pair of these kernel sentences the PS-rules have generated Tense so that we have the difference between *The doctor examines John* and *The doctor examined John*. Yet in the form *the doctor to examine John* there is no tense, and this part of the sentence could equally well have been generated from the kernels *The doctor examined John* or *The doctor examines John*. We select Tense, past or present, in the PS-rules but when we apply the generalized transformation we have to delete it. The issue is the same as with *John was killed* – elements are generated by the PS-rules and then deleted because they are not wanted. This is clearly most unsatisfactory.

This problem can be handled in a way similar to that of the

element Passive. For it is not only important that this element triggers off the obligatory transformation to generate the passive sentence. It is also important that the element itself is deleted by these obligatory transformations. A sentence that contained the symbol Passive, would not be a grammatical sentence. Passive is, therefore, what is known as a 'dummy' symbol: although it may be generated by the PS-rules it must be deleted by the operation of the obligatory T-rules.

The same device can be used to solve the problem of the sentence we have been discussing. Tense too is a dummy which may be rewritten as past or present and subsequently as a grammatical formative, -*ed* or -*s* or zero (*liked*, *likes*, *like*), or alternatively may be deleted by the operation of a transformaton such as the one that generates *I persuaded the doctor to examine John*.

A slightly different solution is required for *John was killed*. For the active form the PS-rules do not generate *Someone*, but a dummy which may be symbolized as $\triangle$. The passive sentence is thus generated from $\triangle$ *killed John* (or more strictly, of course, from the underlying terminal string). The rules state that this dummy must be deleted in the passive, giving us *John was killed*. It is not deleted in the active as this would generate *Killed John as a grammatical sentence. But the conventions state that any sentence that contains any dummy symbol is 'filtered out', i.e. rejected as an ungrammatical sentence. If the final output of the rules is $\triangle$ *killed John* this string is simply eliminated.

This whole approach is particularly well suited to handle generalized transformations. In the more discursive exposition in 4.1 I spoke several times of 'embedding', but there is in fact no place for embedding in the earlier form of the theory; it is merely that two sentences are conjoined. What we need to say is that one sentence is an element within another. This is very simply done if we make all the choices in the phrase structure and also have available the notion of dummy symbols. All we need to do is to generate by the phrase structure rules a symbol that can subsequently be replaced by a sentence. The obvious symbol is the letter S′ which stands for 'sentence', with a dash to show that it is not the same one as we began with. Thus for *I intended the doctor to examine John* and *I persuaded the doctor to examine John* we have to begin with strings:

$$I + past + intend + S'$$
$$I + past + persuade + the + doctor + S'$$

S' is deleted when it is replaced by the sentences to be embedded; obligatory transformations then apply to generate the required sentences.

The device is simple; it shows exactly where a sentence is to be embedded into another and is totally in accordance with traditional (and largely acceptable) views on subordination. Two technical terms may be noted again. The embedded sentence is called the 'constituent'; the sentence into which it is embedded is called the 'matrix' (see p. 141).

In the later form of the theory there is also an attempt to solve the very difficult problem of the restrictions on the co-occurrence of items within a sentence. These seem to be of two kinds. First there are those that exclude *The piano plays Casals*, *I drank the bread*, *The idea cut the tree*. These are essentially lexical restrictions – the impossibility of the co-occurrence (or what many of us have called the 'collocation') of some words with others, in specific grammatical relationships. The second type of restriction is one that makes it impossible to say *I ate that he was coming*. *He elapsed the man*. Here it is not a matter of the incompatibility of pairs of words, but that certain words (here verbs) do not enter at all into certain grammatical constructions. Thus EAT cannot be followed by *any* kind of embedded sentence ('subordinate clause') and ELAPSE cannot be followed by *any* NP, not simply *the man* and a few others (it never has an object but is an intransitive verb). These two kinds of restrictions are dealt with by two kinds of rules – 'selectional' rules, which handle the co-occurrence of wholly lexical items, and 'strict sub-categorization' rules, which handle the occurrence of items in grammatical contexts.

The treatments of these two kinds of restrictions have much in common. Basically the suggestion is that in the lexicon (the dictionary) words shall be marked as having certain features which indicate their restrictions. This is, in effect, what traditional dictionaries do, in some degree, at least in so far as grammatical restrictions are concerned. A verb is marked *tr.* (transitive) or *intr.* (intransitive) which means that it will or will not be followed by an NP. The suggestion is that a similar device shall be used to cover not only a much wider set of grammatical restrictions but also the purely lexical ('collocational') ones as well.

Let us consider first strict sub-categorization (the second of the two kinds of restriction). We want to indicate that EAT will occur with a following NP (its object). We want, in effect, to say that a verb that can be followed by an NP is 'transitive'. This could be shown by simply writing a rule something like

$$V \rightarrow \text{Transitive}/ \underline{\quad\quad} \text{NP}$$

This is read as 'Rewrite V as transitive in the context "before NP"' (the dash shows the context in which the symbol occurs). We must then make an entry in the dictionary that shows that EAT has the feature transitive with the convention that only a verb with this feature can replace V in the context indicated. This will ensure that only transitive verbs such as EAT will be selected in the context of a following NP. But we have many other contexts too. Some verbs, e.g. BECOME, occur before NPs and also before adjectives. Others, e.g. BELIEVE, occur before NPs and 'subordinate' sentences and so on. Our dictionary (lexicon) has to indicate for each verb the context into which it can occur (and, incidentally, it must also show that it is a verb). So we might have dictionary entries such as:

> eat $[+V, + \underline{\quad} \text{NP}]$
> became $[+V, + \underline{\quad} \text{Adjective}, + \underline{\quad} \text{NP}]$
> believe $[+V, + \underline{\quad} \text{NP}, + \underline{\quad} \text{that S}']$

The $+V$ shows that each item is a verb and the other entries clearly specify the contexts in which it may occur. But each of these points is indicated by treating them as positive features of the different verbs. The set of features that are thus assigned to each lexical item form what is known as a 'complex symbol' or CS for short. We now have to say that the selection of a verb in terms of its grammatical context is made by means of specifying these features. This is simply achieved by a rule (a PS rule) that rewrites V as a CS in certain environments, e.g.:

$$V \rightarrow CS/ \underline{\hspace{1cm}} \left\{ \begin{array}{l} NP \\ \text{Adjective} \\ \text{that } S' \end{array} \right.$$

This says that we can select only those verbs which have certain specified features: before a following NP (EAT, BECOME, BELIEVE); before an adjective (BECOME); and before *that* with a sentence (BELIEVE). This is, of course, only a tiny fragment of our grammar. The grammatical restrictions are manifold and complex, but the principle is the same for them all.

The selectional rules work in a similar fashion. But the verbs now have to be selected not with regard to grammatical construction but to the nouns that follow or precede them (their 'subjects' or 'objects'). The relevant features of the noun seem to be such that can be described as 'Abstract', 'Animate', 'Human', etc. Thus FRIGHTEN and KICK will not be followed by abstract nouns (we cannot say *He frightened the thought* or *He kicked the hockey*). FRIGHTEN must be followed by an animate noun, but KICK need not be – *He kicked the table* but not *He frightened the table*. REMEMBER is not preceded by an inanimate noun (*The garden remembered* is impossible). This means that we first have to specify the nouns in terms of such features, i.e. the nouns themselves must be rewritten as complex symbols, and then the verbs must be further specified in terms of the environments which include the features of the nouns. The dictionary must show, for instance, that THOUGHT and HOCKEY are abstract and that GARDEN and TABLE are inanimate. This can be done by a set of rules similar to those above, but using minus signs as well as plus signs to indicate negative features (thus —Animate means Inanimate; this is simpler than writing +Inanimate which would fail to indicate that Animate and Inanimate are a pair of opposites). Thus a simplified entry would be:

thought [+N, +Abstract, —Animate]

house   [+N, −Abstract, −Animate]
man   [+N, −Abstract, +Animate]

(There would be further specification of man as Human, but this raises some more complex problems that are impossible to discuss here – that Human implies Animate and that therefore to specify both Human and Animate would be redundant.) Now we must add features to the verbs – features which are stated in terms of features of the noun – that, for instance, a particular verb can only occur with a following noun that has the feature −Abstract. Thus for FRIGHTEN instead of merely having the entry:

frighten   [+V, +——NP]

which indicates that it is transitive (a strict sub-categorization feature), we write:

frighten   [+V, +——NP, + [+Abstract] Aux ——Det
                                      [+Animate]]

The additional section says that this verb has the feature that it occurs in contexts in which it is preceded by its auxiliary and an element (an NP) which is itself marked as having the feature abstract and in which it is followed by a determiner and an element (an NP) which is marked as having the feature animate. This shows it can occur in the sentence *The thought frightened the boy* but not **The boy frightened the thought* (since *boy* does not contain the feature abstract and *thought* does not contain the feature animate).

In spite of the similarities between the two kinds of rule, they are clearly different in their purpose. Apart from the fact, however, that selectional rules are wholly in terms of lexical items while strict sub-categorization rules involve grammatical contexts, there is a further point. With the strict sub-categorization rules the context within which they have to be stated is one that is dominated in the PS-rules by a single symbol. For instance, the rules about transitive verbs having objects, or verbs such as EAT not being followed by embedded sentences, relate to the element VP and its expansion to V and NP etc. There is no similar limitation of the context for selectional rules, since they may hold between the first NP and the V (the subject and its verb, which excludes *The cloud cut the tree*) for these are not dominated by a single symbol; their common 'ancestor' is S which is rewritten as NP + VP (only subsequently is VP expanded into V + NP).

A more fundamental development in the later form of the theory concerns the relation between semantics and deep structure. If we return to some of the examples in 4.1 it will be apparent that deep structure often accounts for semantic differences that cannot be accounted for in surface structure. The two possible meanings of *The shooting of the hunters* becomes clear once we investigate their deep structure, and the same is true of the contrast between *He is easy to please* and *He is eager to please*. Quite clearly, then, transformational grammar is far more 'semantics-sensitive' than any kind of phrase structure grammar.

It is only a little step further to suggest that deep grammar ought to go even 'deeper' and will thus be identified with semantics. We can, it is suggested, account for the similarity of meaning of

> *He cut it with a knife*
> and   *He used a knife to cut it*

in terms of identical 'deep' structure. On such an analysis the occurrence of *with* in one sentence and *used* in the other are merely features of the surface structure. Similarly, we can establish the semantic relationship between *kill* and *die* by interpreting *kill* as a 'surface' structure representation of *cause to die* so that *The dog killed the rat* is generated from a deep structure of the kind *The dog caused the rat to die*.

Although this seems to be no more than an extension, perhaps a logical extension, of transformational grammar, it is in fact much more. This can be shown by looking at the models in a simple diagram form. According to Chomsky the grammar consists of three components, the syntactic, the semantic and the phonological. The syntactic component generates an infinite set of structures which are then RELATED by the semantic and phonological components to meaning and sound. The syntactic component is thus central and the semantic and phonological components are 'purely interpretive'. We can illustrate the model as:

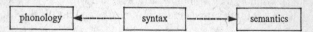

If, however, we agree that deep structure is identical with semantics it follows that the model is somewhat different. It is instead:

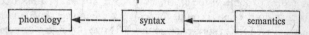

The different direction of the right-hand arrow indicates that we have to begin with semantics (=deep structure) and proceed from there to the syntax and then only to phonology. A more sophisticated approach still asks why we should move in this direction, i.e. from meaning to sound, and suggests that we ought to go in either direction with syntax in the middle, i.e.

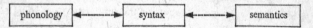

This as we saw in the very first chapter is a plausible model in purely abstract academic terms. How far it can be strictly formalized is not yet clear.

The deep structure semantics approach may seem attractive, but it faces most of the criticisms of traditional notional grammar. The difficulty is that if there are no restraints on what can or cannot be said in deep grammar, then to say that deep grammar is semantics is merely to give a new name to semantics. Linguists have for a long time sought to achieve a satisfactory theory of semantics, but because of the complex heterogeneous nature of meaning have largely failed.

Nevertheless some very interesting speculation has come out of the new approach. One of the most fascinating is what has become known as 'case grammar', associated with the name of the American linguist Charles Fillmore. The theory is based on the fact that we can, for instance, say *John broke the window*, *The hammer broke the window*, *John broke the window with a hammer* and even *The window broke*. What is apparent from this is that in surface structure, relations of subject and object do not seem in any way to indicate deep structure relations. Thus, although we are talking about John as the one who did the breaking, the window as the item that was broken and the hammer as the instrument which was used, all three can appear as the subject of the sentence. Fillmore's solution is to talk of these deep relations in terms of 'cases' so that *John* is agentive, *hammer* is instrumental and *window* is objective. In addition to these three he also requires dative, factitive and locative. Dative is needed for the obvious example of *to John* in *I gave the book to John*. Factitive is required for objects, etc., resulting from the action of the verb (*He painted a picture*) and locative, for example, *Chicago* or *in Chicago* in *Chicago is windy* or *It is windy in Chicago*.

The objective case is the 'semantically most neutral case' – its role depends on the verb itself. The agentive and dative cases are restricted to animate objects and the instrumental to inanimate ones. Different verbs fit into different case-'frames', e.g. OPEN into [___ O], or [___ O + A], or [___ O + I] or [___ O + I + A] with the remarkably different surface representations as in:

> *The door opened,*
> *John opened the door,*
> *The wind opened the door,*
> *John opened the door with a chisel.*

Verbs with similar meaning require different cases. KILL may have an agentive or an instrumental or both (*The man killed him, The sword killed him, The man killed him with a sword*), but MURDER always has an agentive since we do not say *The sword murdered him* though it can occur with both agentive and instrumental (*The man murdered him with a sword*).

This is a very crude outline. Other cases are to be added and have, in fact, already been added (Fillmore has recently modified his theory and his terminology). But there are many difficulties ahead, both in establishing what cases are required and also in the relationship between the deep grammar and the surface grammar. Indeed it is by no means clear, as I said earlier, that this is part of grammar at all. But it is important and interesting and it is to the credit of TG that it has stimulated such speculation.

What the future holds is by no means clear. Some linguists believe that they will be able to discover in deep structure the universal features of language. My own view is that this is rather like the alchemists' search for the philosopher's stone and that just as chemistry turned away from this kind of speculation to the detailed examination of chemical substances, so too linguistics will concentrate in greater detail upon the phenomenon of language itself. We have the scientific resources in the shape of computers and electronic equipment for speech analysis (even if we have still a long way to go). More importantly, perhaps – and this is what this book has been about – we now have sufficient theoretical understanding of the structure of language to make the use of such devices worthwhile.

Appendix A Gender in English

1. English has no gender: the nouns of English cannot be classified in terms of agreement with articles, adjectives (or verbs).

2.1 There are in English pairs of words of the type *stallion/mare, ram/ ewe, boar/sow, uncle/aunt, brother/sister*. But this is a lexical feature, not a grammatical one – related to sex, not gender. We ought to talk of these, then, in terms of 'male' and 'female' not 'masculine' and 'feminine'.

2.2 English has a suffix -*ess* used in, for example, *authoress, princess, duchess*. But this too is a lexical feature. It is not regular, since we have no **teacheress, *doctoress, *kingess*, etc., and it is not even regular morphologically. This is a matter of derivation, but not of grammatical gender.

2.3 Within the same lexical area we have names for small creatures – *foal, lamb, piglet*. There is often a quartet – the generic name, the name of the male, the name of the female and the name of the young (*sheep, ram, ewe, lamb*), though there are fewer distinctions in some cases (*dog* is generic and male, *cow* usually generic and female, *foal* and *colt* distinguish two kinds of young horse, and there is also *filly*). Note that here too there is a very irregular kind of derivation, *piglet, duckling, gosling*.

3.1 The choice of the pronouns is almost entirely a matter of sex – *he* refers to male, *she* to female and *it* to sexless objects or optionally to animals even when their sex is known. If we divide up the words in English according to the pronouns used we find not three classes but seven since some words are referred to by two or three of the pronouns:

he	*man, boy, uncle*
she	*woman, girl, aunt*
it	*table, chair, tree*
he, she	*doctor, teacher, cousin*
he, it	*bull, ram, boar*

> *she, it*   *ewe, sow, ship*
> *he, she, it*   *cat, dog, thrush*

There is one odd man out here – *ship*, and we could have added *car*, *boat*, *engine*. It could be argued that since these are sometimes referred to as 'she' that English has gender, since this is not a matter of sex but of the arbitrary kind of classification found in French *la porte*, etc. But, first, these are very few in number (and we should not wish to build a grammatical category on a few examples) and they belong to a clearly defined class of mechanical things. We can add to this class, and in recent years *plane* and *hovercraft* have been added. This is not then a matter of grammatical gender at all but simply that *she* is used for females and mechanical objects (a class defined semantically).

3.2 The pronouns do not involve any restrictions within sentences since we may have *The boy lost his hat* or *The boy lost her hat*. But there would seem to be restrictions with *-self* since we find *The boy himself* . . . and *The boy hurt himself* not **The boy herself* . . . or **The boy hurt herself*. But this is still accounted for in terms of the sex reference of the pronouns which equally makes the following sentences impossible, unlikely or at least difficult to interpret:

> **The boy hit her own foot*,
> **The boy soon recovered from her accident*,
> **The boy felt a severe pain in her leg*.

Appendix B Number in English

1. English clearly has number in *cat/cats*, *man/men*, etc., and the concord restrictions (a) with verbs *The man comes*, *The men come* and (b) with demonstratives *this man*, *these men*.
2. One slight anomaly is that the present tense forms of the verb are not simply divided morphologically into singular and plural. The division is rather between the 'third person singular' and the rest – *He comes* vs. *I come*, *they come*. The only forms which divide simply into two morphological groups are those of the past tense of BE – *was* and *were*, *I was*, *they were* (*you* presumably can be regarded as a plural form even when it refers to a single person).
3. Morphologically the spoken and the written forms of the noun differ with regard to number classification (see p. 31).
4.1 Number in English is closely associated with a category that the traditional grammar books have largely missed – that of 'countable'/'uncountable' nouns (sometimes called 'count'/'mass'). The distinction is between words such as *cat*, *book*, *road* on the one hand, and *butter*, *petrol*, *bread* on the other. The chief differences grammatically are that the uncountables generally have no plural forms (*butters, *petrols, *breads) and that they do not occur with the indefinite article *a* or *an* (*a butter, *a petrol, *a bread). The contrast is in fact seen clearly in *bread* and *loaf*. The unfortunate foreigner who does not know that *bread* is an uncountable is liable to say 'Can I have a bread?' or 'There were two breads on the table'. In both cases, of course, he could have used LOAF and been grammatical. It is not, however, only the indefinite article that is involved in the countable/uncountable distinction. In addition there is the possibility of no article at all and also of the 'weak' form of 'some' (phonetically [səm]). Countables do not occur (in the singular) without an article, though uncountables do – *Butter is . . .*, but not **Cat is . . .* Uncountables alone occur with the weak form of some, *Would you like some bread?*, but not **Would you like some cat?* (Notice, however, that there is a strong form [sʌm] which does occur with countables – *Some cat has stolen the fish*, or Winston Churchill's

famous *Some chicken, some neck.*) We can illustrate the distinction of uncountable and countable in a table (using ø – zero – to mean 'having no article'):

	a	some ([səm])	ø
cat	√	—	—
butter	—	√	√

4.2 It is, however, possible to 'switch' countables into uncountables and vice versa. We could say *Would you like some giraffe?* to people who eat giraffe, or *A petrol I like very much is Brand X.* Countable nouns, that is to say, may be treated as uncountables if they are regarded as food and uncountable as countable when the meaning is 'a kind of . . .' But the semantics alone is not enough, as shown by *bread/loaf*, or by the fact that we cannot say *a soap* meaning 'a cake of soap'; it is a purely linguistic fact that BREAD and SOAP are uncountable and LOAF countable. Some words belong to both classes, e.g., CAKE *Would you like a cake? Would you like some cake?* (where *loaf* and *bread* are, respectively, the corresponding forms).

5. Some singular nouns ('collectives') are commonly used with plural verbs – *The committee have decided. Engalnd have won the World Cup.* Note, however, that while the verb is plural the demonstratives cannot be. We cannot say **These committee have decided.*

6. Some nouns have no singular – *scissors, trousers, pliers,* etc. All are semantically 'pairs'. These raise an interesting point with the numerals. It might be thought that numerals above *one* can all be used with plural nouns (*three cats, seventy dogs,* etc.). But these plural forms cannot be used with any numerals since we have no **one scissors* or **ten scissors,* etc. But they CAN be used with the plural forms of the demonstratives – *these scissors.*

7. There are some anomalous plural forms, especially *police* and *clergy.* These are unlikely with numerals – **thirty police* would usually be rejected in favour of *thirty policemen* and also unlikely with plural demonstratives, **these police.* They are then rather like the form *committee* used with plural verbs ('collectives'). Note, however, that *people* is in all respects plural (*these people, thirty people,* etc.), and so, too, probably is *cattle.*

8. A minor anomaly is provided by *a dozen* which functions just like *twelve* – *a dozen eggs* (note that *a score, a gross,* do not function in this way). Similarly, *a lot of* functions like *many* – *a lot of men are . . .,* and *kind of,* rather like *such these kind of people* (though this may be thought 'sub-standard').

Appendix C Tense in English

1. Morphologically English has two tenses only, as exemplified by *He likes/He liked*, *He takes/He took*. These are most plausibly referred to as 'present' and 'past'. Other verbal categories, the perfect, the progressive, etc., are achieved by the use of the auxiliaries BE and HAVE.

2. There is, then, a real sense in which English has NO future tense. There are ways of referring to future time, but this is no more a justification for a future tense than the fact that we have ways of referring to near and far (*here/there*) is evidence of a 'spatial' tense.

2.1 The paradigm *I shall, thou wilt (you will), he will*, then *we shall, you will, they will* is purely a grammarian's invention. *I will, we will* and especially the contracted *I'll, we'll* are as much part of the pattern as *I shall, we shall*. Careful investigation has shown that there is no evidence that *I shall, we shall* are the forms regularly used.

2.2 *Shall* and *will* are modal auxiliaries functioning exactly as *can* and *may*. If we establish them as makers of an English tense we ought equally to recognize tenses for the other modals.

2.3 *Will* is used for functions other than future time reference:

> *I'll come, if you ask me.* (willingness)
> *She'll sit for hours.* (habit)
> *That'll be John.* (probability)
> *Oil will float on water.* (general truth)

Note in particular the syntactic contrast of *will* for future and *will* for willingness in:

> *John will come tomorrow.* (futurity)
> *If John comes ...*
> *John will come tomorrow.* (willingness)
> *If John will come ...*

Will then has futurity as only one of several meanings. Similarly, *shall* is used also for threat or promise. *You shall have it tomorrow.*

2.4 There are other ways of referring to future time:

The progressive	*I'm flying to Paris tomorrow.*
going to	*I'm going to ask you a question.*
The simple present	*Term starts on Monday.*
about to	*He's about to speak.*

Going to is particularly important. It differs phonetically from the progressive form of *go*. Contrast:

> *I'm going to London.*
> *I'm going to talk.*

The latter but not the former can be [gənə].

2.5 All these points militate against the traditional view of *will* and *shall* as makers of the future. Why these? Why any future? If meaning is the test, then, it has been suggested, nouns have tense – *ex-wife* is past, *fiancée* future and *grandfather* pluperfect!

3. English past tense does not refer only to past time. It has two other functions.

3.1 Clearly the past tense IS used for past time reference in e.g.

> *He came yesterday.*

Notice, however, that we have also a past progressive (i.e. forms that are past *and* progressive),

> *He was coming yesterday,*

a past perfect,

> *He had come the day before,*

and even a past perfect progressive

> *He had been coming the day before.*

But *came, was, had* mark these all as past (with past time reference).

3.2 The past tense is also used in reported speech in accordance with a 'sequence of tenses' rule:

> *He said he went to London every day*

(his words were 'I go to London every day').

The use of *went* here is determined solely by the use of the past tense form *said*; it does not itself indicate past time, and in many languages a past tense form would NOT be used. Notice, however, that we can use a present tense form if the speaker wishes to indicate that the reported statement is still true:

> *The ancient Greeks discovered that the world is*
> *round, but the Romans maintained that it was flat.*

(We could replace *is* by *was* here, but we cannot replace *was* by *is* without implying that the world is flat.)

3.3 The past tense is often used only to indicate 'tentativeness', improbability or impossibility. There are, perhaps, three separate uses of this kind. First, in statements and questions it is more tentative or even more polite:

> *I wanted to ask you something.*
> *Could you pass me the salt.*

Secondly, it is used with 'impossible' wishes:

> *I wish I knew.*
> *I wish I had one.*

Thirdly, it is used for unreal conditions. Compare:

> *If John comes, I shall leave.*
> *If John came, I should leave.*

The verbs in the second sentence are past tense; the difference in meaning is that in the second there is an assumption that the condition will not be fulfilled – it is 'unreal'. There is no point, then, in talking of 'conditional' forms of the verb; English has no special conditional forms, but uses tense to distinguish real and unreal conditions.

3.4 From this it also follows that English has no subjunctive. What is sometimes referred to as the subjunctive is in fact merely the past tense form in impossible wishes or in unreal conditions (*I wish I knew*, *If John came* . . .). One form that might seem to belie this is that it seems to differ from the past tense form in *were* in *If I were* . . . as compared with *I was there yesterday*. But the remarkable thing here is that it is not *were* that is exceptional but *was*. The paradigm of *I/you/he/we/they were* is wholly regular, since with all other verbs there is only one past tense form – *I/you/he/we/they loved*. *Was* then is the odd man out, a special form used with singular pronouns and nouns when tense is used for PAST TIME reference. Clearly then there is no evidence of a special 'subjunctive' form. The other form sometimes referred to as the subjunctive is in fact the uninflected 'simple' form:

> *God save the queen.*
> *If that be so ...*

But this is the same as the 'infinitive', the 'imperative' and the present tense form without -*s* (except for BE). Here English comes closest to being an 'isolating' language (p. 55) in its verbal system, and subjunctive is essentially a category belonging to highly inflected languages!

Further Reading

Some of the general topics in Chapter 1 are further discussed in R. A. Hall, *Linguistics and Your Language*, New York, 1960. Another useful introductory book is Randolph Quirk, *The Use of English*, 1962.

Introductions to linguistics are to be found in H. A. Gleason, *An Introduction to Descriptive Linguistics* (Revised Edition), New York, 1961. R. A. Hall, *Introductory Linguistics*, Philadelphia, 1964. C. F. Hockett, *A Course in Modern Linguistics*, New York, 1958. R. H. Robins, *General Linguistics: An Introductory Survey* (Second Edition), 1971. These deal in various ways with the topics of Chapters 2 and 3, but the American books, in particular, largely adopt the theoretical approach of Chapter 3.

Transformational-generative grammar has its origins in Noam Chomsky's *Syntactic Structures*, The Hague, 1957. Chomsky's *Aspects of the Theory of Syntax*. Cambridge, Mass., is relevant, but will prove very difficult reading for the non-specialist. A good introductory book is John Lyons, *Chomsky*, 1970.

On English H. A. Gleason, *Linguistics and English Grammar*, New York, 1965, is useful. The reader might also look at the author's work on the English verb, F. R. Palmer, *A Linguistic Study of the English Verb*, 1965.

Index

(This index refers only to pages on which the more important topics are explained or discussed in detail.)

*Some other books published by Penguins are
described on the following pages.*

Mind the Stop

G. V. Carey

'The best brief guide to punctuation I know' –
J. Donald Adams in the *New Yorker*

'*Mind the Stop* is a readable book, but, better
still, it is one that will readily help those writers
who take a pride in their craft' – *Writer*

'This excellent little book quickly disposes of the
common fallacy that punctuation should follow
the breathing-spaces appropriate to reading
aloud, and insists that its true function is to make
perfectly clear the construction of written
words' – *English*

'Adopts a personal style of demonstrating the
subject which certainly appeals to one and
emphasizes the practical nature of the
compilation' – *British Printer*

'All who object to slovenly language will read
the book with gratitude' – *Modern Languages*

'Presents in a fresh and entertaining way
material that might easily have been treated
pedantically' – *The Times Educational Supplement*

New Horizons in Linguistics

Edited by John Lyons

'The faculty of articulated speech', as Darwin once wrote, 'does not in itself offer any insuperable objection to the belief that man has developed from some lower form.' Perhaps not: but it makes a mighty big difference.

In recent years the scientific study of language has been pushed to a point where its findings necessarily interest philosophers, psychologists, sociologists, anthropologists and others concerned in any way with words and their meaning. This collection of essays by seventeen British, German, and American experts in various fields of linguistics forms a running report on the directions being pursued today in each branch of the discipline. These outlines of recent research and new theories in phonology, morphology, syntax, and semantics provide a highly authoritative introduction for first-year students and inhabitants of neighbouring intellectual worlds.

However, though Professor Lyons has not assembled a mere primer of linguistics, any reader who can regard such words as 'phonemic groups' or 'morphemic segments' as stimulants rather than narcotics will find this an intriguing study of a subject which is rightly attracting more and more interest.

Linguistics

David Crystal

'It is impossible to conceive of a rational being, or of a society, without implying the existence of a language. Language and thinking are so closely related that any study of the former is bound to be a contribution to our understanding of the human mind.'

Popular interest and the evident importance of language as the principal means of communication between people, interests, creeds and nations have promoted linguistics, largely in this century, from an amateur study to a widespread academic discipline.

David Crystal shows here how the scientific study of language grew up separately and distinctly in Europe and America. Following the brilliant but ill-recorded work of Ferdinand de Saussure he traces six 'ages' in the development of linguistics, each with its dominant, and abiding, theme. His central chapter discusses, one by one, phonetics, phonology, morphology, 'surface' syntax, 'deep' syntax, and lastly semantics.

Dr Crystal's book makes a novel and lively introduction to a significant subject which today concerns not only psychologists, sociologists and philosophers, but teachers, interpreters and even telephone companies.